I0143256

JOURNAL OF BIBLICAL LITERATURE

MONOGRAPH SERIES, VOLUME II

PRAYER IN THE APOCRYPHA AND PSEUDEPIGRAPHA

A Study of the Jewish Concept of God

by

NORMAN B. JOHNSON

Professor of Religion
Knox College, Galesburg, Illinois

*A grant from The Lucius N. Littauer Foundation has supplied
the funds needed for printing this book.*

SOCIETY OF BIBLICAL LITERATURE AND EXEGESIS

222 NORTH FIFTEENTH STREET
PHILADELPHIA 2, PENNSYLVANIA

Copyright, 1948, by

SOCIETY OF BIBLICAL LITERATURE AND EXEGESIS

ISBN 0-89130-172-0

TABLE OF CONTENTS

PREFACE

THIS study of prayers excludes blessings and curses because they are different from petitions through being automatic and irrevocable rather than dependent on the will of deity. Prayers of thanksgiving and praise, however, provided they mention a boon, are handled along with petition and intercession, for probably the hope of continued or repeated favor is normally not far from the surface of the mind. Only pure praise is handled as a somewhat different type of prayer.

Virtually every section is introduced by a glance backward into the Old Testament and is concluded with a glance forward into the New Testament or the early rabbinic prayers. These allusions backward and forward serve only as abutments for the intertestamental bridge; no effort is made to do justice to the earlier and later prayers.

For translations from the Apocrypha and Pseudepigrapha I am indebted to Charles and his collaborators;[1] and for those from the early rabbinic prayers, to Oesterley's *Jewish Background of the Christian Liturgy*, a book from which I have drawn freely. I have altered these translations only to the extent of introducing consistency in capitalization and punctuation. Biblical quotations are from the American Standard Version (1901), and are used by permission of the International Council of Religious Education.

May I take this opportunity for expressing my sincere gratitude for the generous help given by two members of the Department of Oriental Languages and Literatures at the University of Chicago: Dr. Ralph Marcus, who suggested the topic of intertestamental prayers and read the manuscript critically; and Dr. Samuel I. Feigin, who gave advice on certain of the Old Testament references.

This work is dedicated to Gene.

[1] Though I have profited from Goodspeed's clear interpretation of the Greek, I feel it inadvisable to quote his American translation of the Apocrypha alongside Charles's archaic translation of the Pseudepigrapha.

1

LIST OF ABBREVIATIONS

Add. Esth. — Additions to Esther
Ahab. — Ahabah
Ahik. — Ahikar, Story of
Apoc. Mos. — Apocalypse of Moses
Arab. — Arabic
Arist. — Aristeas, Letter of
Arm. — Armenian
As. Mos. — Assumption of Moses
Bar. — Baruch
Bel. — Bel and the Dragon
Ben. — Benediction
Ber. — Berakoth
Did. — Didaché
En. — Enoch
Ep. Jer. — Epistle of Jeremy
E. R. E. — Encyclopedia of Religion and Ethics
Esd. — Esdras
Geul. — Geullah
Jub. — Jubilees, Book of
L. A. E. — Life of Adam and Eve
Mac. — Maccabees
Mart. Is. — Martyrdom of Isaiah
Mish. — Mishnah
P. Azar. — Prayer of Azariah

Pir. Ab. — Pirke Aboth
P. Man. — Prayer of Manasses
Ps. Sol. — Psalms of Solomon
Sib. — Sibylline Oracles
Sir. — Sirach, Book of
S. L. A. E. — Slavonic Life of Adam and Eve
S. T. C. — Song of the Three Children
Sus. — Susanna
Syr. — Syrian
T. A. — Testament of Asher
T. B. — Testament of Benjamin
T. D. — Testament of Dan
T. G. — Testament of Gad
T. Iss. — Testament of Issachar
T. Jos. — Testament of Joseph
T. Jud. — Testament of Judah
T. L. — Testament of Levi
T. N. — Testament of Naphtali
Tob. — Tobit, Book of
T. R. — Testament of Reuben
T. S. — Testament of Simeon
T. Z. — Testament of Zebulun
Wisd. — Wisdom of Solomon

INTRODUCTION

AN ancient Jewish rabbi once wrote: "It can be discovered from the prayers of a man whether he be religiously cultured or uncultured" (Tosephta, Ber. I, 6). He might have said, more specifically, there is no better index of a man's understanding of God than his prayers. Learn what a man prays for, and you see at once the scope he assigns to God's power. Learn, in the second place, what inducements a man offers God for the fulfilment of prayer, and you perceive much concerning the character the man assigns to God. And finally, learn what manner of response this man expects — for instance, whether immediate or mediated — and you are in a position to infer whether the individual conceives of God as being manlike or utterly different, close at hand or distant, intimate or austere and despotic.

This indirect approach to theology is dependable because through it we catch a man off guard. What he tells us directly about his concept of God is often warped by his desire to force consistency into his own thinking, and is often prejudiced by the very questions he is trying to answer. But if, unknown to him, we can invade the privacy of his chamber and hear the spontaneous outpouring of his own prayer, then we can truly overhear his beliefs. Nothing reveals them more honestly than does (1) the catalog of what he prays for, (2) the way he tries to induce God to grant the petition, and (3) the manner of response he expects.

This study of prayers as an index to a man's or a people's understanding of God, is most effective when applied to a monotheistic faith. Polytheism, especially a highly departmentalized polytheism such as that of the Roman Empire, is a poor seedbed for spontaneous prayer. When a man goes to a different temple for the satisfaction of each of his special needs, such as healing or victory, he does not have to phrase his own prayer; the fixed formula is usually adequate. In fact, words are often

3

unnecessary when he has come to the proper shrine. But the monotheist, believing that one God satisfies all needs, must voice his prayer explicitly. So prayers constitute a rich source of insight into the faith of a people like the Jews, whose orthodox belief, from the time of their great prophets, has been at war in defense of the unity of God.

As would be expected, spontaneous prayers have characterized Judaism from the legendary period of the patriarchs to the present. "Down to the last days of the first temple, there were no formal prescribed prayers — not even a general command to pray."[2] Gideon's natural conversations with God are typical (Judg. 6:14 ff.). Though the prophetic Psalms became crystalized as part of the temple liturgy, and though the synagogues developed a prayer liturgy, never did *ex tempore* prayer lose its prominent role in the religion of the Jew. To the contrary, the spontaneous outpouring of petition, lament, praise, and thanksgiving received a new impulse when the destruction of the temple in A. D. 70 deprived the Jew of his sacrifices and threw added weight upon prayer along with almsgiving and the study of the Law.[3] It is these living prayers, and not the liturgies, that give us our best key to an appreciation of the Jews' evolving concept of God.

For the prayers of the two or three centuries which elapsed between the composition of the latest book of the Hebrew Old Testament and the earliest book of the New Testament, our richest sources are the Apocrypha and the Pseudepigrapha. The Apocrypha, or "Hidden Writings," are fourteen Jewish religious books which were not part of the Hebrew canon, but which found their way into the Septuagint, the Greek Old Testament compiled by Greek-speaking Jews of Alexandria, Egypt. The Latin Bible of the Roman Catholic Church includes the fourteen Apocrypha; but Protestant Bibles, from the time of Martin Luther onward, either have relegated these books to a subordinate section between the Testaments or have omitted them altogether. The Pseudepigrapha are similar Jewish books which

---

[2] Felix Perles, "Prayers, Jewish," *E. R. E.*, vol. X, p. 191.
[3] Ralph Marcus, *Law in the Apocrypha*, p. 98.

gained acceptance in neither the Hebrew canon of Palestine nor the Greek Septuagint of Alexandria. As their name indicates, many of them are "writings falsely attributed" to famous men of the past, such as Moses or Enoch. But the term "Pseudepigrapha" might apply equally well to certain of the Apocrypha: for instance, Esdras, Baruch, and the Wisdom of Solomon.

While, of course, the prayers imbedded in the Apocrypha and Pseudepigrapha are not actually spontaneous, they are probably not far from it. Therefore, we may feel reasonably sure of the reliability of our data when we analyze these prayers through the three captions suggested above: aims, inducements, and expected responses. The findings will help bridge the gap between the prayers of the Hebrew Old Testament on the one hand and, on the other, the early rabbinic prayers and the prayers of the New Testament. But beyond the prayers themselves we shall see emerging in clearer detail the concept of God which, in varying forms, dominated the mind of the Jew during the intertestamental age.

LIST OF THE APOCRYPHA AND
THE PSEUDEPIGRAPHA

THE APOCRYPHA	THE PSEUDEPIGRAPHA

THE APOCRYPHA

First Esdras
First Maccabees
Second Maccabees
Third Maccabees
The Book of Tobit
The Book of Judith
Ecclesiasticus, or the Book of Sirach
The Wisdom of Solomon
First Baruch and the Epistle of Jeremy
The Prayer of Manasses
The Prayer of Azariah and the Song of the Three Children
The History of Susanna
Bel and the Dragon
Additions to Esther

THE PSEUDEPIGRAPHA

The Book of Jubilees
The Letter of Aristeas
The Books of Adam and Eve:
  The Life of Adam and Eve
  The Slavonic Life of Adam and Eve
The Apocalypse of Moses
The Martyrdom of Isaiah
First Enoch
The Testaments of the Twelve Patriarchs: Reuben, Simeon, Levi, Judah, Issachar, Zebulun, Dan, Naphtali, Gad, Asher, Joseph, Benjamin
The Sibylline Oracles
The Assumption of Moses
Second Enoch
Second Baruch
Third Baruch
Fourth Ezra
Psalms of Solomon
Fourth Maccabees
Pirke Aboth, from the Mishnah
The Story of Ahikar:
  Versions: Syriac A, Syriac B, Arabic, Armenian
Fragments of a Zadokite Work

This list follows Charles by including Third Maccabees among the Apocrypha, and Fourth Ezra among the Pseudepigrapha. Though neither Pirke Aboth nor the Story of Ahikar is a Pseudepigraphon, Charles includes both because "they were used, at all events partially, by Jewish readers within this period."[4]

[4] R. H. Charles, *The Apocrypha and Pseudepigrapha*, vol. II, p. iv.

I. THE AIMS OF THE PRAYERS

A. Help in Warfare

"And Jephthah vowed a vow unto Jehovah, and said, 'If thou wilt indeed deliver the children of Ammon into my hand, then it shall be that whatsoever cometh forth from the doors of my house to meet me, when I return in peace from the children of Ammon, it shall be Jehovah's, and I will offer it up for a burnt offering' " (Judg. 11:30, 31).

Whatever may have been the name the early Hebrews gave to their tribal god, surely he was a god mighty in battle. Prayers for success in warfare held an important place among their petitions from nomadic days down through the Old Testament and into the intertestamental period. Naturally, when the son of Sirach wrote, "Let me now hymn the praises of men of piety, of our fathers in their generations" (Sir. 44:1), he remembered how Joshua "called on the Most High God, when he was in sore straits and his enemies around him" (Sir. 46:5); how it was in response to a prayer by Samuel that the Lord "subdued the garrisons of the enemy and destroyed all the princes of the Philistines" (Sir. 46:16–18); how David vanquished Goliath by a warlike prayer (Sir. 47:5); and how the people of Jerusalem called on the Lord for help when Sennacherib laid siege to their city (Sir. 48:20).

The Apocryphal Book of Judith was written to prove that insistent prayer and unswerving fidelity to the Law can enable even a woman to overcome the most powerful of armies. When Holofernes, captain of the Assyrian host, marched against Palestine, every man of Israel cried to God (Judith 4:9). Again and again as the peril neared and then encircled the stronghold at Bethulia, the villagers prayed (Judith 6:19, 21; 7:19). Before Judith set out for Holofernes' camp with only her maid beside her, she urged the people to plead with God for her success

7

(Judith 8:17). She herself prayed, "Make my speech and deceit to be their wound and stripe, who have purposed hard things against thy covenant" (Judith 9:13); and the elders of the village asked God to make her designs a defense for Israel (Judith 10:8). Having easily won the trusting adoration of the Assyrian captain by her beauty and her wiles, Judith prayed at the captured spring (Judith 12:8). In the very tent of Holofernes she said in her heart, "O Lord of all power, look in this hour upon the works of my hands for the exaltation of Jerusalem" (Judith 13:4). Grasping the hair of drunken Holofernes' head, she drew his own scimitar and said, "Strengthen me, O Lord God of Israel, this day" (Judith 13:7). Judith then carried the enemy's head to the elders of her village and bade them, "Praise God, who . . . hath destroyed our enemies by my hand this night" (Judith 13:14). The people, seeing the gory prize, uttered a prayer of praise: "Blessed art thou, O our God, which hast this day brought to nought the enemies of thy people" (Judith 13:17). Judith's exultant psalm epitomizes the theme of her story: "O Lord, thou art great and glorious, marvelous in strength, invincible" (Judith 16:13). The virile traits of the ancient warrior god still dominated the character of God as the writer of these prayers imagined him.

The academic and pious Letter of Aristeas, though far removed from the dust of battles, nevertheless reveals in one passage the tenacity with which even the refined Jewish scholar held to this early concept of God. Ptolemy Philadelphus, at one of the great banquets which he gave in honor of the learned translators of the Septuagint, asked how he could become invincible in war. The reply was unequivocal: Call upon God (Arist. 193).

First and Second Maccabees contain many war-prayers, for these two books relate the story of the last successful effort of the Jews to battle the foreign oppressor: the history of the revolt of the Maccabean princes against the Seleucid kings of Syria in the second century B. C.

The author of First Maccabees represents Judas, the first of the princes, as praying that the foe's 60,000 men may cringe in fear before his own 10,000 (I Mac. 4:32), or praying in the spirit of Old Testament warriors: "Crush this army before us today" (I Mac. 7:42). The rebel commands his soldiers to pray before attacking (I Mac. 4:10), and on another occasion they do so of their own accord (I Mac. 3:44–53). During a charge against the enemy, Judas's men sound their trumpets and cry aloud in prayer (I Mac. 5:33), and after a battle they praise heaven for their victory (I Mac. 4:24). When the Syrian captain Nicanor threatens the temple, the priests pray, "Take vengeance on this man and his army, and let them fall by the sword" (I Mac. 7:38). Judas's successor, his brother Jonathan, commands prayer when his army is encircled (I Mac. 9:46) and himself prays again when ambushed by the foe (I Mac. 11:71).

Second Maccabees repeats the familiar refrain of prayer for aid in warfare (II Mac. 1:8; 8:14, 15; 12:28; 13:10–12; 13:14; 14:15; 15:26) or praise of God for the victory (II Mac. 1:11; 8:27; 10:38; 15:29). But in Second Maccabees the prayers are often more impassioned than in the calm First Maccabees, where God is quietly referred to as "heaven." The author of Second Maccabees praises God for the violent and bloody death of King Antiochus (II Mac. 1:17). This writer represents Judas and his men as calling on God to "manifest his hatred" of the wickedness of the foe (II Mac. 8:4), to fight on the rebels' side (II Mac. 10:15, 16; 12:36), and to be "the enemy of their enemies" (II Mac. 10:26). Thus a passionate character is attributed to God.

But the most striking difference between the war-prayers of First Maccabees and those of Second Maccabees appears in the baroque supernaturalism of the latter. Evidently the author of Second Maccabees was a Pharisee, for often his narrative introduces angels and the miraculous. Judas beseeches the Lord to send some valiant angel to save the strongholds which the Syrians are besieging (II Mac. 11:6), or, as in King Hezekiah's time, to send an angel to carry fear and terror before the patriot army (II Mac. 15:23). When charging horsemen appear in the sky over Jerusalem during the hated King Antiochus' second attack on Egypt, the Jews pray that the strange manifestation may betoken good for the cause of their own forces (II Mac. 5:4). Finally, Judas and his men, during their attack upon a walled town, call on "the great Sovereign of the world, who without rams and instruments of war had laid Jericho low in the days of Joshua" (II Mac. 12:15). Such prayers indicate a belief that God can be induced to intervene miraculously.

In summary, when "suddenly the alarm of war was heard" (Ps. Sol. 1:2 , the loyal Jew still turned to God as Lord of hosts. Doubtless if the Apocrypha and Pseudepigrapha included accounts of Pompey's invasion in 63 B. C. and of Titus's devastating campaign of A. D. 70, we would find war-prayers again. But these would be almost the last. To many of the Jews, intrigue and revolt seemed futile even before Rome's legions first marched through Palestine and especially after Titus looted and destroyed the temple. Historic forces beyond the control of the Jew diverted his mind from arms and toward a new heaven and a new earth, a gift of God and of his Messiah, here or elsewhere. After Titus, the Jew seldom had occasion to pray the prayers of Judas Maccabeus.

B. DELIVERANCE FROM ENEMIES OTHER THAN THOSE OF WAR

"And the Egyptians dealt ill with us and afflicted us and laid upon us hard bondage: and we cried unto Jehovah, the God of our fathers, and Jehovah heard our voice" (Dt. 26:6, 7).

From earliest days the Jew has prayed to God as his deliverer from those who persecute or oppress him. Of God's aid in this regard the devout Jew is reminded twice daily by the closing words of the "Hear, O Israel": "I am Jehovah your God, who brought you out of the land of Egypt, to be your God: I am Jehovah your God" (Num. 15:41).

Prayers for deliverance from the oppressor are abundant in the Apocrypha and Pseudepigrapha. In one of the oldest stories appropriated by the Jews, the sage Ahikar, a victim of slander, was hiding in a dungeon from King Sennacherib, who thought that Ahikar had been duly beheaded. The fugitive prayed for God's help (Ahik., Arab. 4:17) and asked his friend the executioner to pray for him (Ahik., Syr. 4:18, 19). When finally Egypt threatened Assyria, and Sennacherib was in dire need of his former counsellor, the crafty executioner brought Ahikar forth alive. Joyously both the ruler and the sage praised God for the deliverance (Ahik., Arab. 5:12, 15; 6:29).

An appendix to Sirach contains a prayer of thanksgiving by one who attributes to God his escape from the execution which threatened to overtake him when he was slandered in the presence of the king: "From the power of Sheol thou didst deliver my foot; thou didst preserve me from the scourge of a slanderous tongue" (Sir. 51:2).

In the Book of Judith, Achior, commander of the Ammonite allies of the Assyrians, in explaining to Holofernes why the Israelites were so hard to defeat, told him of how in Egypt they cried to God and he delivered them, as he was always ready to do (Judith 5:12).

The Book of Jubilees depicts the Hebrews praising and thanking God during their first observance of the Passover in Egypt, for their deliverance from bondage was at hand (Jub. 49:6).

Fantastic Third Maccabees contains a story of how Ptolemy Philopator, a cruel Egyptian ruler, tried in vain to destroy a group of Jews by exposing them in the arena to the frenzy of a herd of drugged elephants. The people whom he would have destroyed, however, prayed for God's succor day after day and thanked him day after day for his mercy as he stalled the designs of the persecutor. The prayer of the aged priest Eleazar tipped the scales in favor of complete deliverance at last, and even the wicked king gave thanks (III Mac. 5–7).

The author of the Apocryphal additions to Esther tells of a dream in which Mordecai heard his people cry out to God when they were in danger of persecution and death through the influence of the treacherous Haman in the court of the Persian monarch (Add. Esth. 11:10). So Mordecai himself prayed for God's deliverance of the Jews (Add. Esth. 13:8–17).

Our final instance is a prayer in which a sage praises God for the many occasions on which he has rescued the faithful by the very means which he has employed to punish their enemies (Wisd. 10:20–12:25).

In the New Testament, Jesus, agonizing in Gethsemane, beseeches God to take the cup of death from him if possible (Mt. 26:39; Lk. 22:42. Cf. Mt. 26:53; Jn. 12:27; Heb. 5:7).

The church prays God to release Peter from prison (Acts 12:5); and Paul asks his friends in Thessalonica to intercede for his deliverance from "unreasonable and evil men" (II Th. 3:1, 2).

This "defending hand" characterized the Jewish concept of God prior to, throughout, and after the intertestamental period. Sometimes the doctrine took a narrow nationalistic turn, as in Esther.[5] More frequently it veered over toward a highly ethical dogma concerning the justice of God's deliverance or punishment.[6] In the Messianic forms, the "defending hand" may well be considered a sublimation of God's warlike trait in a time when warring was futile.[7]

C. A SAFE JOURNEY

"And Jacob vowed a vow, saying, 'If God will be with me and will keep me in this way that I go, and will give me bread to eat and raiment to put on, so that I come again to my father's house in peace, and Jehovah will be my God, then this stone which I have set up for a pillar shall be God's house; and of all that thou shalt give me I will surely give the tenth unto thee'" (Gen. 28:20–22).

It would be surprising if among a nomadic people like the early Hebrews we should find no prayers for a safe journey. One of the most famous of these prayers is this vow which Jacob made as he set out from Bethel to seek a wife in Paddan-Aram. Likewise Ezra, centuries later, proclaimed a fast and prayers for a safe return of the exiles from Babylon to Jerusalem (Ezra 8:21–23).

The Apocrypha and Pseudepigrapha continue this tradition. For instance, when Tobias is leaving for his long trek, Tobit, his aged father, giving him some advice that reminds us of that given by Polonius, includes an injunction to pray God for protection on the journey (Tob. 4:19); and Tobias, turning homeward after many fortunate adventures, praises God for prospering him on the odyssey (Tob. 11:1).

In the Book of Jubilees, Abram prays not only for guidance as

---

[5] See I, I below.
[6] See I, K, 4 below.
[7] See I, K, 5 below.

to where he shall settle, but also for God's protection on the way (Jub. 12:21). Then, having come into his new country, he thanks God for bringing him safely from Ur to Canaan (Jub. 13:7. Cf. Jub. 22:27), and later gives God thanks for granting him a safe return from his strange adventure with Sarai in Egypt (Jub. 13:15).

The author of the Wisdom of Solomon acknowledges in his apostrophe to God that on the long passage through the wilderness it was God who watched over the wandering Hebrews; he it was who gave the cloud overhead, the dry land beneath their feet in the Red Sea, and the quail which they ate. The same journey which brought death to the Egyptians brought the Hebrews in safety to the land of the covenant (Wisd. 19:1–12). This author extends to the seas God's guidance of the traveler: "Even in the sea thou gavest a way, and in the waves a sure path, showing that thou canst save out of every danger, so that even without art a man may put to sea" (Wisd. 14:3, 4).

Though the New Testament contains no explicit prayer for safe travel, we can feel little doubt that this is one of Paul's aims when he kneels with his friends at the beach near Miletus or Tyre and prays before setting sail (Acts 20:36; 21:5).

Such prayers imply a belief that God is not restricted to one place.

D. RAIN

"Jehovah, when thou wentest forth out of Seir, when thou marchedst out of the field of Edom, the earth trembled, the heavens also dropped, yea the clouds dropped water. The mountains quaked at the presence of Jehovah, . . . the God of Israel . . . . From heaven fought the stars, from their courses they fought against Sisera. The River Kishon swept them away, that ancient river, the River Kishon. O my soul, march on with strength. Then did the horse hooves stamp by reason of the prancings, the prancings of their strong ones" (Judg. 5:4, 5; 5:20–22).

This Song of Deborah, which is probably one of the most ancient portions of the Old Testament, makes it clear that the prophetess believed God had saved the Hebrews by a heavy rainstorm which flooded the valley of the River Kishon and caused the chariots of the enemy to bog down.

Solomon, in his prayer for the dedication of the temple, prayed that whoever faced the temple and made petition for rain should win his request, provided he was penitent for such sins as might have brought on the drought (I K. 8:35, 36); and the prophet Jeremiah pleaded with God for rain when the earth was cracked (Jer. 14).

In all the Apocrypha and Pseudepigrapha, however, there is only one prayer for rain. When the Assyrians had invested Bethulia and had cut off the village from its water supply, one of the elders of the Bethulians asked Judith to pray that the Lord send rain to fill their cisterns (Judith 8:31). The reason for the scarcity of such prayers is not that the Jews ceased to think of God as the giver of rain; there is abundant evidence that the Jews conceived of him as exercising complete control over all of nature. Probably, however, the established agricultural festivals, offerings, and prayers seemed adequate to provide the necessary rains.

The New Testament makes only a passing allusion to one rain-prayer, that of Elijah in the time of King Ahab (Jas. 5:17, 18).

In the early rabbinic prayers known as the Eighteen Benedictions, rain is mentioned twice. Both instances are clearly subordinate to prayers for abundant harvests:

"Thou art mighty for ever, O Lord, . . . that causest the wind to blow and the rain to descend; thou sustainest the living with mercy, thou quickenest the dead" (Ben. II).

"Bless us, O Lord our God, in all the work of our hands, and bless our years and give dew and rain upon the face of the earth, and satisfy the world and its fulness with thy goodness" (Ben. IX).

If the rain-prayer is praise and thanksgiving, like Benediction II above, there is still room for the belief that God is orderly in his control of nature. If, on the other hand, the prayer is a petition for rain on a specific occasion, the petitioner is very likely to think of God as being arbitrary in marshalling natural forces. The Jew evidently preferred the dignity of the prophetic

concept: "If ye shall hearken diligently unto my commandments . . . I will give the rain of your land in its season" (Dt.
11:13, 14). This is the morally conditioned mean between the
one extreme of a blind natural order and the other extreme of an
arbitrary God.

E. Food and Drink

"Look down from thy holy habitation, from heaven, and bless
thy people Israel and the ground which thou hast given us, as
thou swarest unto our fathers, a land flowing with milk and
honey" (Dt. 26:15).

Thus closes one of the two oldest formal prayers recorded in
the Old Testament: Deuteronomy 26:5–10, 13–15.[8] These
prayers are to be recited on the occasion of offering the firstlings
and the tithes, and their ultimate purpose is obviously God's
continued favor upon the efforts of the farmer. The productivity
of the earth is in God's hands, as Hosea very dramatically
reminds Israel, who, like the harlot Gomer, has run after her
lovers, the Baalim, in the false belief that it is they who give
her the bread, flax, oil, and wine which actually come from God
(Hos. 2:1–13).

In all the Apocrypha and Pseudepigrapha there is not a single
prayer that is aimed directly at success in agriculture. The
fertility of fields, like the regular coming of the rain, was well
cared for by the agricultural festivals and offerings and by the
traditional prayers which accompanied them.

In the Pseudepigrapha there are, however, allusions to prayers
before meals. The Letter of Aristeas relates that when Ptolemy
Philadelphus dispensed with his own sacrifices and prayers
before a great dinner and asked the oldest of the Jewish priests
to say grace, the aged scholar "rose up and made a remarkable
prayer: 'May Almighty God enrich you, O King, with all the
good things which he has made . . . .' " (Arist. 184, 185). This
prayer is not so remarkable after all, for it is only a paraphrase
of the familiar prayers recited even in pre-Christian days by all

---

[8] Felix Perles, "Prayer, Jewish," *E. R. E.*, vol. X, pp. 191, 192.

devout Jews at mealtime: "Blessed art thou . . . who createst the fruit of the vine, . . . who bringest forth bread from the earth, . . . who createst the fruit of the tree, . . . who createst the fruit of the ground" (Mish., Ber. 6:1).

Another reference to prayers before meals is found in the Sibylline Oracles: "Happy shall those men be throughout the earth who shall truly love the mighty God, blessing him before eating and drinking, staunch in their godliness" (Sib. IV, 24–26).

The New Testament's two versions of the Lord's Prayer both include the request for daily bread (Mt. 6:11; Lk. 11:3). Jesus gives thanks for the loaves and fishes before feeding the multitude (Mt. 14:19; 15:36; Lk. 9:16; Jn. 6:11), for the bread and wine at his last supper with the disciples (Mt. 26:26, 27; Lk. 22:17, 19; I Cor. 11:24), and for the bread he breaks while visiting *incognito* in the home at Emmaus (Lk. 24:30). Paul observes the inveterate Jewish custom even in the midst of a storm at sea (Acts 27:35).

The prayer at mealtime is but one step removed from a prayer for the continuance of God's blessing on field, orchard, vineyard, and garden. The mealtime prayer, being an expression of thanks and praise subsequent to the gift, is of higher rank than a petition, but probably suggests to many minds the hope which is so frankly voiced in an early rabbinic prayer, the ninth of the Eighteen Benedictions: "Prosper . . . this year with every kind of produce, keeping from it every kind of destruction and want."

F. Health

"Wherefore recover thou me, and make me to live" (Is. 38:16).

Just as King Hezekiah pleaded with God for the restoration of health, so the aged Tobit, though once he had prayed for death as a release from his blindness, poverty, and disgrace (Tob. 3:2–6), later gave God credit and thanks for the restoration of his sight (Tob. 11:14, 15). In the same story, Raguel made petition in behalf of his daughter Sarah and her groom Tobias that they might live to the end in health (Tob. 8:17). Sirach and the Letter of Aristeas advise that we pray for healing and for protection from disease (Sir. 38:9; Arist. 233). In response to

Jacob's prayer, the Lord healed Gad's disease of the liver (T. G. 5:9) and relieved Reuben's illness which came as a punishment for lying with Bilhah (T. R. 1:7; 4:4). Simeon, finally penitent for his bitter jealousy of Joseph, prayed for the restoration of his withered hand, for God had punished him in this way lest the hand strike Judah for letting Joseph go alive (T. S. 2:13). Probably the most daring of these petitions was Joseph's, when he ate enchanted bread and asked God to prove his power by letting no evil come of the meal (T. Jos. 6:7). The tragic poet Theodektes prayed for the restoration of his eyesight when he realized that his blindness was due to his planning to use some of the incidents of Jewish holy writ in one of his plays (Arist. 316). In Second and Fourth Maccabees we find parallel stories about Heliodorus and Apollonius, each of whom threatened to plunder the treasures deposited in the temple at Jerusalem and was struck down by an angel on horseback, only to be saved by the high priest, who prayed for the recovery of the intruder lest the Syrian king suspect foul play on the part of the Jews (II Mac. 3:31; IV Mac. 4:13). Our final instance of prayer for healing occurs in the Life of Adam and Eve, where the first man asks his wife and his son Seth to pray for oil from the tree of life, that they may anoint him and relieve him of his death pains (L. A. E. 36:1, 2).

Early rabbinic prayers follow suit. The Hashkibenu, which is the second prayer following the recitation of the "Hear, O Israel" each evening, embraces among its aims protection from pestilence, and the second of the Eighteen Benedictions includes in its assurances: "With great mercies thou dost heal the sick."

The New Testament recommends the healing of disease through prayer, confession, and anointing (Jas. 5:14–16). Peter prayed in order to raise Tabitha from the dead (Acts 9:40); Paul thrice besought God to remove the "thorn" from his flesh (II Cor. 12:8), and he prayed for the healing of the father of Publius on the Isle of Melita (Acts 28:8); furthermore, the whole group of the disciples asked God for the power to heal (Acts 4:29, 30).

All such prayers attribute to God an absolute control over our bodies: health and illness are subject to his will. Since there is no concept of a mechanistic natural law, these healings are not to be considered supernatural; they constitute only a remarkable manifestation of God's perpetual power.

G. DEMON RIDDANCE

The orthodox Jewish tradition of the Old Testament looks askance upon the belief in demons. Even as late a writing as the Prologue to the Book of Job presents Satan as an agent of God's will. The Persian and Hellenistic ages, however, planted in the Jewish mind the seed of demonology, and early instances of the belief appear in Tobit and in the Life of Adam and Eve. When Tobias' destined bride prays for either death or release from the reproaches of her father's maids, she is indirectly pleading for riddance from the demon Asmodeus, who has slain her seven husbands, each on his wedding night (Tob. 3:11–15); and on Raphael's advice, youthful Tobias, the eighth groom, uses a prayer as a support to the rite performed against the demon (Tob. 6:17; 8:7). Both Eve and Adam pray that they be freed from "that devil" (L. A. E. 17:1–3; S. L. A. E. 35:1); but here we find a devil who is really a fallen angel, only one false step removed from the divinely approved status of Satan in the Prologue to Job. In all cases, God can exercise dominion over the evil spirits (Jub. 10:6).

The early rabbinic prayers now extant, adhering strictly to the orthodox tradition, have virtually no traffic with demonology, but the first Christians, both Jewish and gentile, embraced this popular belief which was current throughout the masses of the Graeco-Roman world. Jesus himself, sharing the belief, said to the disciples concerning the demon which had possessed the epileptic boy, "This kind can come out by nothing save by prayer" (Mk. 9:29). There can be little doubt that this belief in demons, especially a belief in a realm of demons ruled by a prince, constitutes a possible threat to the doctrine of God's perpetual omnipotence, for demonology may lead in the direction of the sort of dualism that dominates the religion of the Zoroastrians. However, the very existence of prayers for demon riddance testifies to a continued faith in God's omnipotence.

H. Procreation

"And Abram said, 'O Lord Jehovah, what wilt thou give me, seeing I go childless?' " (Gen. 15:2)

The Apocrypha and Pseudepigrapha contain numerous instances of prayers for the birth of sons. Ahikar voiced the petition in vain (Ahik., Syr. A 1:4, 5); but Abraham praised his Creator for the promise of holy seed which would "become like him who had made all things" (Jub. 16:26), and at his death thanked God for that seed, placing two of Jacob's fingers on his eyes (Jub. 23:1). Though Leah felt it necessary to plead for a second son (T. S. 2:2), she later had the opportunity to bless God for a fourth (T. Jud. 1:3). Her rival Rachel, unproductive for twelve years after Joseph's birth, prayed, as did Jacob, and Benjamin was born (T. B. 1:4, 5). Jacob also prayed that his childless son Judah be given progeny (T. Jud. 19:2). The most striking instance, however, is Joseph's intercession: when Potiphar's wife tried to mother Joseph on the pretext that she had no son of her own, he "prayed to the Lord and she bore a male child" (T. Jos. 3:7).

The prayer for progeny naturally extends its scope to include the woman's prayer for aid in childbirth. Eve, when in labor, cries out, "Pity me, O Lord, assist me" and urges Adam to pray for her (L. A. E. 19:2; 20:2—21:3).

The New Testament continues the prayer for sons. An angel says to Zacharias, "Thy supplication is heard, and thy wife Elisabeth shall bear thee a son, and thou shalt call his name John" (Lk. 1:13).

The unpredictability of conception probably tended to stimulate a belief in God's wilful control.

I. Establishing and Restoring the Nation

The ancient song-prayer of Deborah not only celebrates the death of the hostile general Sisera and shouts to God, "So let all thine enemies perish, O Jehovah" (Judg. 5:31); it also immortalizes the victorious beginning of that gradual process by which the people began to think of God as a national, rather than as a tribal deity. Samuel was the prophet who carried this movement through to its logical culmination in the establishing of a theocratic kingship for united Israel.

The conquest of northern Israel by the Assyrians and of Judah by the Babylonians did not destroy Hebrew nationalism; many a prayer like that of the eightieth Psalm pleaded for the restoring of the nation. Though the second Jerusalem was slow in regaining strength, the Maccabean revolt against the Seleucid tyrants in the second century B. C. generated a violent resurgence of the national spirit. This spirit infuses many of the prayers of the Apocrypha and Pseudepigrapha. Shortly before the revolt, the son of Sirach prayed: "Make an end of the head of the enemy's princes that saith: 'There is none beside me!' Gather all the tribes of Jacob, that they may receive their inheritance as of old" (Sir. 36:10, 11). In quieter but equally nationalistic spirit he pleaded that there might be peace in Israel in his days and through the days of eternity (Sir. 50:23 and textual note).

Throughout the changing fortunes of the Maccabean wars, of Pompey's conquest, and of the devastation wrought by Titus, ardent patriots composed their restoration prayers, sometimes innocently disguising these prayers as belonging to previous eras, lest the incumbent ruler consider the writing seditious, or the Jewish reader consider it trifling (II Mac. 1:23–29; I Bar. 4:20, 21, 27, 36, 37; T. Jos. A. 19:1–4; As. Mos. 3:9; 4:1–6; Ps. Sol. 11:1–9).

The theological basis for the nationalism of such prayers was usually a belief that the Jews are God's chosen people. The Book of Jubilees represents Abraham as praying in behalf of his sons that they may be to God "a chosen nation and an inheritance from amongst all the nations of the earth from henceforth unto all the days of the generations of the earth, unto all the ages" (Jub. 22:9), and the Wisdom of Solomon closes with a prayer of thanksgiving for God's special favor to his chosen nation: "In all things, O Lord, thou didst magnify thy people, and thou didst glorify them and not lightly esteem them; standing by their side in every time and place" (Wisd. 19:22. See also II Bar. 48:18–20).

Many nationalists in time of exile or oppression turned to God in the hope that he would reestablish for Israel the old Davidic dynasty: "Behold, O Lord, and raise up unto them their king, the son of David, . . . and he shall judge the tribes of the people that has been sanctified by the Lord his God" (Ps. Sol. 17:23–28).

But some of these nationalistic prayers undermined the foundation of their own nationalism by proclaiming the justice of God's judgments against Israel, as the great prophets had done, who never forgot that the covenant was morally conditional — that God's special favor was contingent upon Israel's obedience to the Law. The oppressive Syrian or Roman was an agent of the divine will. Thus the Jew recognized in God a universal power for justice, rather than a sponsor of one nation (I Bar. 2:11–3:8; IV Ezra 9:29–37; Ps. Sol. 8).

A second influence that tamed the nationalism of the Jewish faith was a genuine respect for the power of Rome. Although the twin prayers for the saving of the life of the enemy Heliodorus or Apollonius' are clearly nationalistic — the ultimate aim of the prayers being to avoid the king's suspicion of foul play by the Jews — other prayers seem to betray a dying of faith in God's concern for Israel's political independence. Writing shortly after the final destruction of the temple, the author of First Baruch, for instance, represents the ancient exiles as urging the Jews of Jerusalem to "pray for the life of Nabuchodonosor, king of Babylon, and for the life of Baltasar his son, that their days may be as the days of heaven above the earth" (I Bar. 1:11). To the Jews of that day these names could have suggested none other than those of Vespasian and his son Titus. Furthermore, Rabbi Hanina, somewhat earlier, had said, "Pray for the peace of the kingdom; for, except for the fear of that, we should have swallowed up each his neighbor alive" (Pir. Ab. 3:2). Both writers were evidently anxious that the Jews should accept Rome's sovereignty and should put out of mind all thought of national independence. This trend, which dominates the New Testament (e. g., I Tim. 2:1, 2), reflects a change in the concept of God's

⁹ See I, F above.

purpose. Jews who became Christians and many Jews who did not accept the Nazarene, had no thought of political freedom when they prayed "Thy kingdom come." For them the national ideal had been transformed into a universal ethical ideal, sometimes of this world, sometimes of another.[10] If certain of Jesus' followers hailed him as the earthly Davidic Messiah on the occasion of his triumphal entry into Jerusalem (Mt. 21:9; Mk. 11:9, 10; Lk. 19:37, 38), his crucifixion put an end to their expectation.

The early rabbinic prayers, however, cling to a shadow of the old hope for restoring the nation. The eleventh of the Eighteen Benedictions, for instance, says without equivocation: "Restore our judges as in former times, and our counsellors as in the beginning, . . . and do thou alone reign over us." This hope for the restoration may be detected also in the tenth and the nineteenth Benedictions and in the prayer which is recited morning and night after the "Hear, O Israel" (Geul.). In order to do justice to such lingering nationalism, we must remember that, for the Jew who takes his great prophets seriously, the hope for national restoration is contingent upon penitence and holds the gate open to the gentile proselyte.

J. THE TEMPLE AND ITS SACRIFICES

Many prayers in the Apocrypha and Pseudepigrapha cluster around the desecration of the temple by Antiochus Epiphanes in 168 B. C. and the destruction of the temple by Titus in A. D. 70. To understand the urgency of these prayers, it is necessary to know how much the Jew had at stake in the sacrifices and in the temple itself. This knowledge, in turn, throws light on the Jewish concept of God.

In the centuries preceding the great reforms led by Josiah in the seventh century B. C., private sacrifice and prayer had gone hand in hand. On the mountain east of Bethel, Abram "builded an altar unto Jehovah and called upon the name of Jehovah" (Gen. 12:8). But Josiah's reforms banned all

---

[10] See I, K, 5 below.

sacrifices save at the temple in Jerusalem. Thereafter the temple was not only the house of prayer toward which the Hebrew turned his face whenever he prayed (I K. 8:30), but also the focus for the offerings which had previously given added efficacy to prayers at the local shrines. Little wonder, therefore, that the author of Daniel, when Antiochus had desecrated the temple, represented the prophet as praying in Babylon concerning the first temple, which lay in ruins: "Cause thy face to shine upon thy sanctuary that is desolate" (Dan. 9:17).

Shortly after the rededication of the temple upon Judas's victory, an Apocryphal writer composed the Song of the Three Children, which became part of Daniel in the Septuagint. The song is an outburst of praise, in which all creation rejoices over the restoration of the house of God (S. T. C. 28–68). Likewise in First Esdras, Zerubbabel's brothers offer a prayer of thanksgiving when they learn that they are to be allowed to return to Jerusalem from Babylon and to rebuild the temple (I Esd. 4:62); and Levi, in the Book of Jubilees, praises God for a dream concerning the priestly honors which are to belong to him and to his sons (Jub. 32:1). Though set in past eras, these prayers are all expressive of the feelings dominant among the Jews who saw their temple rededicated after Judas's triumph. There may be a similar indirect reference in Third Maccabees: when Ptolemy Philopator threatened in 217 B. C. to enter the Holy of Holies in the temple, the priests and Simon the high priest prayed God to turn the man aside (III Mac. 1:16; 2:1–20).

First and Second Maccabees give direct and undisguised accounts of the temple crises in the time of Judas. When Heliodorus attempted to plunder the deposits in the sanctuary, the priests petitioned God to protect these treasures, which the sanctity of the place was expected to guard (II Mac. 3:15), and the people blessed the Lord for miraculously sending a dreadful rider and two young men to strike down the intruder (II Mac. 3:30). At the time of the actual desecration of the altar by Antiochus, Judas and his men voiced a prayer of lament over the desolation of the temple (I Mac. 4:39, 40), and after the restoration all the people blessed heaven (I Mac. 4:55; cf. II Mac. 10:7). Judas and his followers prayed that there might never be another profanation of the shrine (II Mac. 10:4); but later, as Nicanor swore he would destroy the temple and build a fane to Dionysus on its site, the priests again had to pray for the protection of the holy place (II Mac. 14:34–36), and again Judas's men had reason to thank God when Nicanor lay dead (II Mac. 15:34).

Of course the final destruction of the temple by Titus brought out many a lament, which was often cautiously framed in the events of the remote past. Baruch, comrade of Jeremiah, is said to have told the priests at Jerusalem to throw the keys of the sanctuary into the heavens and to cry out, "Guard thy house thyself, for lo we are found false stewards" (II Bar. 10:18). Ezra himself prayed for mercy in view of the degradation of the temple (IV Ezra 12:48) and had a vision of a woman, Zion, praying for a son, who represents the institution of temple sacrifices (IV Ezra 9:44). The Apocalypse of Moses adds pathos to these laments by pushing the custom of offerings back to Adam himself, who in leaving the garden pleaded with the angels: "I pray you, allow me to take away fragrant herbs from paradise, so that I may offer an offering to God after I have gone out of paradise, that he hear me" (Apoc. Mos. 29:3).

All such prayers reveal a conviction that the temple and its sacrifices were virtually indispensable. The reason why they seemed indispensable was that the Jew believed that God was strongly influenced by the temple ritual.[11] They thought he was moved by its solemn pageantry, provided righteousness accompanied the sacrifices (Job 42:8). So a rabbinic prayer still voiced the hope: "May our eyes behold thy return to Zion" (Ben. XVII).

K. RIGHTEOUSNESS AND JUSTICE

1. *Confession and Forgiveness*

"Against thee, thee only, have I sinned and done that which is evil in thy sight" (Ps. 51:4). The prayer of confession and for forgiveness has deep roots in the past of Judaism. It finds classic expression in Ezra, Nehemiah, and Daniel (chapter 9 of each).

---

[11] See II, B below

Such outpourings proclaim a belief that God is concerned with righteousness and that evil-doing constitutes a direct offense against his will.

The Wisdom of Solomon implies that heathen idolaters, sharing none of this idealism about God's concern for the right, pray for nothing other than material blessings (Wisd. 13:17–19). But we ourselves, says Sirach, should turn to God in prayer over our former sins (Sir. 21:1; 39:5), for he will forgive us (Sir. 17:29; cf. Sib. III, 624–629; IV, 166–170; II Bar. 84:10; Ps. Sol. 9:12) if we honestly intend not to repeat the offense (Sir. 34:26).

The Prayer of Manasses is typical. Opening with praise, it confesses sin, prays for forgiveness and grace, and closes with a doxology. Though attributed to the Judean king who had reacted against the reforms of his father Hezekiah, it may well have been a prayer for general use.

Prayers for forgiveness were often intercessory. The high priest Simon spoke for all the community when he prayed: "Blot out our sins and scatter abroad our offenses" (III Mac. 2:19). Benjamin says in his testament: "Joseph besought our father (Jacob) that he would pray for our brethren, that the Lord would not impute to them as sin whatever evil they had done unto him" (T. B. 3:6). Again, the Babylonian exiles asked Jerusalem to beseech God to turn aside the wrath he felt because of their sins (I Bar. 1:13), and Judas's men even prayed for the forgiving of their slain comrades who had worn idolatrous amulets on their chests (II Mac. 12:41–45). But there can be no prayer for forgiveness at the time of the final judgment (II Bar. 85:12).

As early as pre-Christian times, the Jewish synagogues had as part of the regular liturgy certain prayers for forgiveness (Selichoth) which they had taken over from the temple liturgy.[12] One of the oldest of the liturgical prayers of confession is the Ashamnu ("We have trespassed"), and at least two passages in the Eighteen Benedictions are confessional: "Bring us back in perfect repentance to thy presence" (Ben. V) and "Forgive us, our Father, for we have sinned" (Ben. VI).

[12] W. O. E. Oesterley, *The Jewish Background of the Christian Liturgy*, p. 76.

As for the early Christians, the Lord's Prayer seeks forgiveness; the Didaché refers to prayers of confession (Did. IV, 14; XIV, 4); and the parable of the publican contains the simplest of all prayers for forgiveness: "God, be thou merciful to me, a sinner" (Lk. 18:13; see also Acts 8:22; I Jn. 1:9; cf. Lk. 23:34; Acts 7:60).

It is evident that all these prayers not only look on sin as a direct affront to God, whose will is righteous; they also presuppose a gracious attitude on God's part.

2. *Moral Wisdom for the Petitioner*

"Give thy servant therefore an understanding heart to judge thy people, that I may discern between good and evil" (I K. 3:9). Solomon's prayer for wisdom was one of the forerunners of many of the most highly ethical prayers of the Apocrypha and Pseudepigrapha; for the wisdom sought was moral discrimination, which was significantly regarded as a gift from God.

This is not the crafty sort of wisdom immortalized in the Story of Ahikar. After seeing the superhuman cleverness of Ahikar, who proved he could build castles in the air if Pharaoh would only furnish the material, the proud Pharaoh himself was moved to say, "Blessed be God, who hath made thee perfect in wisdom" (Ahik., Arab. 7:4; 7:19). Here we dip back into a level of wisdom below the rank of the ethical; but Sirach's scholar had reason to thank God for the sort of wisdom men live by (Sir. 39:6; 51:17), which is God's gift to the godly (Sir. 43:30–33). Having specifically identified wisdom with God's Law (Sir. 24:23–27), he is proud to say, "When I was yet young, before I wandered abroad, I desired (wisdom) and sought her out. In my youth I made supplication in prayer; and I will seek her out even to the end" (Sir. 51:13, 14; cf. Sir. 37:15; Wisd. 7:7, 15; 8:21–9:18; IV Ezra 8:6).

Zerubbabel, the guardsman who won the contest of wise sayings, gave God thanks for his victory (I Esd. 4:59, 60). Again, when Ptolemy Philadelphus asked one of the Hebrew translators of the Septuagint what philosophy really is, the scholar replied that philosophy is deliberate, dispassionate, and moderate living;

"but," he added, "we must pray to God to instil into our mind a regard for these things" (Arist. 256). It is a prayer of the Wisdom of Solomon, however, that best epitomizes the belief that God is the source of higher wisdom: "To know thee is perfect righteousness" (Wisd. 15:3). A prayer in the first section of this same book goes so far as to identify wisdom with the Word of God, the Logos, and thus seems to anticipate Philo[13] and the prologue of the Fourth Gospel:[14] "O God of the fathers, and Lord who keepest thy mercy, who madest all things by thy Word, and by thy wisdom formedst man, . . . give me wisdom, . . . that sitteth by thee on thy throne" (Wisd. 9:1, 2, 4). The Wisdom of Solomon, therefore, stands on the threshold of one of the most fertile concepts of Jewish and Christian theology.

Probably the latest of these prayers for divine wisdom is Ezra's petition that he be granted the Holy Spirit as he begins to write (IV Ezra 14:22; cf. Wisd. 7:7). This suggests the baptismal prayer of Jesus, after which the Galilean received the Holy Spirit symbolized by a dove (Lk. 3:21, 22). James urges this sort of prayer when he writes: "If any of you lacketh wisdom, let him ask of God, who giveth to all liberally and upbraideth not" (Jas. 1:5; see also Mt. 11:25, 26; Acts 8:15; I Cor. 14:13; II Cor. 2:14; Eph. 1:15–18; 3:14–19; Philip. 1:9–11; Col. 1:9, 10).

Among the early rabbinic prayers, the Ahabah makes petition for divine wisdom in these typically Jewish words: "Enlighten our eyes in thy Law," and the fourth Benediction says, "Grant us from thee knowledge and understanding and discernment."

Thus the prayers of the Christian and of the Jew alike perpetuate the ancient belief that God is the source of that wisdom which constitutes a guide to the moral life. The mysticism of such a relationship binds man and God very close to each other.

3. Protection from Future Sin; the Gift of Certain Virtues

"He guideth me in the paths of righteousness for his name's sake. Yea, though I walk through the valley of the shadow of death, I will fear no evil, for thou art with me" (Ps. 23:3, 4).

---

[13] R. H. Charles, *Apocrypha and Pseudepigrapha*, vol. I, p. 549, note on IX, 1.
[14] E. J. Goodspeed, *The Story of the Apocrypha*, p. 98.

The vigorous ethical teaching of the Hebrew prophets influenced men to seek not only pardon for past offenses, but also specific aid toward a moral life in years ahead. Sirach prayed for a curb upon his tongue and upon his sensual desire (Sir. 22:27—23:6); Simeon, for freedom from envy against his brother Joseph (T. S. 2:13). Gad advised an indirect prayer for warding off jealousy: "If a man prospereth more than you, ... pray also for him that he may have perfect prosperity .... If he be further exalted, ... offer praise to God" (T. G. 7:1, 2). Often Joseph prayed for protection against the wiles of Potiphar's wife (T. Jos. 3:3; 4:3, 8; 7:4; 8:1, 5), and the Psalmist sought aid against fornication, lying, wrath, and impatience under chastisement (Ps. Sol. 16:7–15). Likewise the New Testament raises a doxology in gratitude for God's power to keep men from sin (Jude 24, 25; cf. II Cor. 13:7).

Others of the intertestamental prayers are positive rather than negative. One of the Septuagint translators, for instance, advised Ptolemy to pray for courage to endure whatever befell him (Arist. 197); another of them urged him to seek generosity as a means of retaining renown (Arist. 226); yet another, to pray that enemies be won over to righteousness through the king's liberality (Arist. 227); a fourth, to pray for utter fidelity to duty, lest ease and pleasure prevail (Arist. 245); and a fifth, of whom the king asked how he could live amicably with his wife, replied that women are headstrong and irrational, and that therefore "it is only by calling upon the help of God that men can steer a true course of life at all times" (Arist. 250, 251). It was also an Apocryphal writer who made Queen Esther plead that God give her courage and eloquence for her crucial audience with the king (Add. Esth. 14:1–19), a petition paralleling the prayer of the Christians for courage to speak the word with all boldness (Acts 4:29). These prayers for virtue go to seed when they change to a proud thanksgiving for virtues already attained, as in the parable of the Pharisee at the temple (Lk. 18:9–14).

The Book of Jubilees, devoted to honoring every Yod and tittle of the Law, says that Moses urged God not to deliver the people into the hands of the gentiles, lest Israel be led astray (Jub. 1:19–21), and in similar vein the Psalmist prays for a strictly moderate share of material blessings, lest privation lead to sin, or an overabundance to transgression (Ps. Sol. 5:18–21). The two prayers may throw some light on a highly controversial clause in the Lord's Prayer: "Lead us not into temptation" (cf. Mt. 26:41; Lk. 22:40).

A writer of the second century B. C. affords early instances of prayers for protection from the corrupting influence of evil spirits. Noah prays that the wicked spirits, the sons of those who had embraced the daughters of men, may not succeed in tempting his sons (Jub. 10:3–6); and Abram, that the evil spirits not lead him astray, or his seed (Jub. 12:20). Somewhat akin is a petition in the second of the prayers which follow the "Hear, O Israel" in the evening: "Drive away the evil one from before us and behind us" (Hashkibenu), and a clause from the Lord's Prayer: "Deliver us from the evil one" — if this be a correct translation of τοῦ πονηροῦ. This concept of evil spirits or of an evil one as the source of temptation stems from a loyal desire never to attach any sort of unrighteousness to the name of God, but there is a problem involved in reconciling the concept with the Jew's unfaltering faith in the sovereignty of God.

4. God's Justice Here and Now

"Hold not thy peace, O God of my praise; for the mouth of the wicked and the mouth of deceit have they opened against me: they have spoken unto me with a lying tongue. They have compassed me about also with words of hatred, and fought against me without a cause" (Ps. 109:1–3).

If God be just, then he will listen to the prayer of the man who is thus wronged (Sir. 35:13): the aim of many supplications is that God prove his justice by defending the upright person here and now. Susanna cries out to God to vindicate her innocence and chastity (Sus. 42, 43), and the Psalmist prays for protection from vicious slander (Ps. Sol. 12).

Equally logical is the assumption that, if God be just, the wicked will be punished. Many Jews expected this punishment to come within the natural lifetime of the offender. When

Judas Maccabeus learned that the men of Joppa had treacherously drowned two hundred Jews, he called on God, "the righteous judge," to enable the Jewish army to exact due punishment (II Mac. 12:6). The Psalmist, lamenting Pompey's lustful plundering, asked God to "turn the pride of the dragon into dishonor" (Ps. Sol. 2:24–29), and, despising the cant of hypocrites, prayed God to bring misery throughout life to all "menpleasers" (Ps. Sol. 4:16–22). The proper manner of divine punishments is mentioned in an apostrophe to God in which the writer of the Wisdom of Solomon declares, "By what things a man sinneth, by these he is punished" (Wisd. 11:16).

The suffering of men who are essentially good is different from mere punishment. "Jehovah trieth the righteous; but the wicked and him that loveth violence his soul hateth" (Ps. 11:5). This belief of the Old Testament Psalmist is seconded in the apostrophe of the Wisdom of Solomon: "When they (the Hebrews) were tried, albeit but in mercy chastened, they learned how the ungodly were tormented, being judged with wrath: for these, as a father, admonishing them, thou didst prove; but those, as a stern king, condemning them, thou didst search out" (Wisd. 11:9, 10). The Pseudepigraphic Psalmist praises God for this chastening, which restrains men from evil (Ps. Sol. 10:1–8). In another prayer of thanksgiving for God's chastening, he declares, "He pricked me as a horse is pricked, that I might serve him . . . . I will give thanks unto thee, O God, for thou hast helped me to my salvation" (Ps. Sol. 16:4, 5). Such chastening prepares the people for the restoration of David's dynasty (Ps. Sol. 18:6).

Judas and his men, preferring to be chastened by God himself rather than by some foe, prayed "that, if ever they should sin, he would chasten them with forbearance, instead of handing them over to blasphemous and barbarous pagans" (II Mac. 10:4). Ezra makes the same plea (IV Ezra 5:29, 30), and a prayer of the Psalmist gives the reason why God's own chastisement is to be preferred: "For thou art merciful and wilt not be angry to the point of consuming us" (Ps. Sol. 7:4).

The frankly confessional prayer of Azariah, acknowledging the full justice of God's punishment of his people, nevertheless entreats the Lord to accept a contrite heart and a humble spirit: "Deal with us according to thy forbearance, and according to the multitude of thy mercy" (P. Azar. 16, 19). This mercy toward those who are at heart loyal though at times they need rods and stripes, is the chief difference between God's disciplinary chastening and his just vengeance.

God's justice in this life demands not only penalties, but also rewards. In the Letter of Aristeas, Ptolemy asked a Jewish scholar how a king "could keep all his possessions intact and finally hand them down to his successors in the same condition. And he answered, 'By praying constantly to God that you may be inspired with high motives in all your undertakings and by warning your descendants not to be dazzled by fame or wealth, for it is God who bestows all these gifts, and men never by themselves win the supremacy'" (Arist. 196). In other words, as the author of the Old Testament Book of Judges contends again and again, material blessings are among God's rewards for the godly. Something of this hope seems to linger in an early rabbinic prayer: "Upon the righteous . . . and upon the proselytes of righteousness, let thy mercies be stirred, O Lord our God; and grant a good reward to all that trust in thy name in truth; and set out our portion with them forever" (Ben. XIII).

In summary, if times were not too bad, the Jew often reverted to his forefathers' hope that God would here and now give just reward to the righteous. But the drama of Job had been written, and Job's skepticism concerning this hope had begun to lay hold on Judaism.

5. God's Justice in a New Jerusalem or in Heaven

"O that thou wouldest rend the heavens, that thou wouldest come down, that the mountains might quake at thy presence . . . to make thy name known to thine adversaries, that the nations may tremble at thy presence" (Is. 64:1, 2).

Repeated shattering of the national hopes of Israel gradually inclined the faith of this indomitable people toward a more remote balancing of the books through some such divine intervention as Isaiah envisioned. When Jerusalem fell before Titus's legions, a prophetic writer using the name of ancient Baruch prayed that God bring a speedy end to this unjust order and that he set up his own kingdom (II Bar. 21:19–26). Enoch taught that only the righteous will survive that awful Day, and that the mighty will vainly plead for respite from punishment (I En. 63). But those who are spared "shall glorify the Lord forever" (T. Jud. 25:5). Tobit's prayer of rejoicing praises God for the universal justice through which all nations are to have access to the New Jerusalem of sapphire and emerald and gold (Tob. 13:7–18; 14:7). According to some prayers, God is expected to exercise direct control over the kingdom (T. S. 6:5); according to others, a Messiah (T. Jud. 24:5, 6) or a Son of Man (I En. 62:9) does the actual saving of the righteous.

Many Jews believed that a sharing of this kingdom necessitated a resurrection of the flesh. The literalness with which the belief was accepted comes out clearly in the barbaric story of a Jewish elder named Razis. When cornered by the enemy he slashed his own body open with his sword, "tore out his bowels, taking both his hands to them, and flung them at the crowds. So he died, calling him who is Lord of life and spirit to restore them to him again" (at the time of the resurrection) (II Mac. 14:37–46).

Only in the later of the Apocrypha and Pseudepigrapha do we begin to encounter allusions to a belief in a blessed state into which a soul may enter immediately after death. The Apocalypse of Moses, for instance, makes the dying Adam say to Eve, "Pray to God till I give up my spirit into his hands who gave it to me. For we know not how we are to meet our Maker, whether he will be wroth with us or be merciful and intend to pity and receive us" (Apoc. Mos. 31:4), and Eve herself, at the moment of death, prays, "God of all, receive my spirit" (Apoc. Mos. 42:8). Ezra explains that, "as the soul from the body departs that it may return to him who gave it," first of all it praises the glory of the Most High; then, if the soul despised the Law, it shall wander in torment of seven ways; but the soul that kept the Law shall enter into seven orders of rest (IV Ezra 7:78–99). Such torment or rest endures till the Day of Judgment. Thus, through a scheme which sounds very much like Zoroastrianism, the Greek belief in the immortality of the soul is dovetailed with the Hebrew doctrine of the resurrection of the flesh; but the object of all three teachings is the same: the demonstrating of God's justice — a universal justice which rises above nationalism and deals with every individual according to his merit.

Jesus evidently had in mind an immediate heaven when with his last breath he cried out, "Father, into thy hands I commend my spirit" (Lk. 23:46; see also Acts 7:59); for he had said to one of the malefactors crucified beside him, "Today shalt thou be with me in paradise" (Lk. 23:43). In addition to this belief, however, the Christians retained the hope of a divine kingdom, for whose early coming they prayed (IV Ezra 2:13, 14). The souls of the Christian martyrs pleaded, "How long, O Master, the holy and true, dost thou not judge and avenge our blood on them that dwell on the earth?" (Rev. 6:10; see also Rev. 16:5, 6; 19:1, 2) and the last book of the New Testament closes with this hope: "He who testifieth these things saith, 'Yea, I come quickly.' Amen, come Lord Jesus" (Rev. 22:20; see also Rev. 11:17, 18; 19:6–8). The only point at which this belief is hard to reconcile with a belief in God's justice is that point at which the Christian prays to thank God for including him among those who are "called" to the kingdom (IV Ezra 2:37).

The rabbinic prayer called the Alenu is an eloquent expression of faith in the coming of a universal kingdom of God beyond any restriction of nationalism: "Therefore we hope in thee, O Lord our God, that we may speedily see the glory of thy might, . . . when the world shall be set right in the kingdom of the Almighty, and all the children of flesh shall call upon thy name."

In brief, the prayers for righteousness reveal the belief that God is characterized by justice tempered with mercy. (1) Prayers of confession look upon all unethical conduct as a direct offense against God's will, while petitions for forgiveness reflect faith in his mercy. (2) In the prayer for moral wisdom is found a conviction that God is the fountainhead of man's moral insight. (3) The quest of security from future temptation sometimes involves the positing of an evil one, lest God's goodness be limited. (4) In prayers for justice here and now, God's mercy emerges to mitigate the penalty for those who are at heart loyal to his will. (5) And finally, the plea for God's ultimate balancing of the books in paradise or in a New Jerusalem is really nothing less than an affirmation of the conviction that God will eventually bring justice, however discouraging the present order may appear.

L. Oracular Response

"Call unto me and I will answer thee, and will show thee great things, and difficult, which thou knowest not" (Jer. 33:3).

It is beyond the scope of this study to review the many ways in which the ancient Hebrews sought oracular responses: the ark, the ephod, the Urim and Thummim, the witch, the seer, the prophet, and direct petition answerable by vision, messenger, or voice. Our prime concern is with the fact that, so far as the Apocrypha and Pseudepigrapha indicate, the Jew of the intertestamental period was more likely to resort to prayer than to mechanical instruments of oracular inquiry. The manner of response is the topic of a later section.

Aristeas relates how the historian Theopompus, after beginning to recover from a month of madness, prayed to learn for what offense he had been punished thus (Arist. 314, 315), and Ptolemy, according to the same author, offered a prayer of thanks to God for a beautiful manuscript of the Jewish Law, which the king thought was truly a book of the oracles of God (Arist. 177).

The great mass, however, of the Apocryphal and Pseudepigraphic prayers for oracular response constitute part of the technique of revelation literature, that is, of apocalypse. A fragment from the Book of Noah preserved in First Enoch represents archangels as praying God to tell them what to do toward curbing the violence of giants born to the daughters of men (I En. 9:4–11). In a series of visions Enoch asks an angel for an explanation of the tree of life (I En. 25:2), the monsters Leviathan and Behemoth (I En. 60:9), the four presences who pray (I En. 40:8), certain astronomical phenomena (I En. 43:3), the Son of Man (I En. 46:2), seven metal mountains (I En. 52:3), the instruments of punishment (I En. 54:4), the scourges (I En. 56:2), the measuring cords (I En. 61:2), the fiery cloud that gave forth laments (I En. 108:5), the tormenting of the prisoners (II En. A 7:3), and the giants with sad faces (II En. A 18:2). After receiving the apocalypse from their father, Enoch's sons praise God for giving them "such a sign through Enoch" (II En. A 68:7). Baruch asks God to interpret the vision of the vine and the cedar (II Bar. 38:1–4) and the vision of the cloud (II Bar. 54:6), to explain the seeming injustice suffered by the righteous (II Bar. 14:1–19), the nature of the resurrection of the dead (II Bar. 49:1–3), and the mystery of a chosen people chastened by the ungodly (III Bar. 1:1, 2). Again, Baruch inquires of an angel concerning the extent and the occupants of the various heavens, concerning the dragon and the monster, and concerning countless other mysteries he encounters in his vision (III Bar. 1:7; 2:4, 6; 3:5; 4:1, 5; et passim). At the close he thanks God for counting him worthy of the revelation (III Bar. 17:3). Finally, Ezra prays God for knowledge about the time of the Last Day (IV Ezra 8:63), about the meaning of his vision of the man from the sea (IV Ezra 13:14–20), about God's reason for his harsh dealings with Israel and his leniency with the heathen (IV Ezra 3:4–36), about God's motive in abandoning his covenant (IV Ezra 4:23), about the reason why the heathen rule a world created for the chosen people (IV Ezra 6:38–59), and about the meaning of his dream concerning the eagle (IV Ezra 12:7–9); and, in a passage probably written by an early Christian, Ezra asks an angel to explain the identity of a tall young man in a vision of Mount Zion and to identify a throng of worshipers on whose heads the young man was placing crowns (IV Ezra 2:44, 46).

While it is of course true that these apocalyptic prayers are purely conventional — that is, merely the usual way of leading up to a revelation from God — the very fact that prayer is chosen as the conventional approach is itself indicative of the dominant rank of prayer among the means of seeking oracular responses.

When Jesus was preparing himself for his apocalyptic ex-

perience on the mountain, prayer was his avenue of approach
to the vision which two of his disciples shared with him (Lk.
9:28–36). Furthermore, when previously he had been faced
with the practical problem of selecting the twelve, he "continued all night in prayer to God," presumably for guidance
in the choice (Lk. 6:12, 13; cf. Acts 1:24–26). As the simple
dignity of the doctrine of God's adequacy gradually permeated
the Jewish mind, it was inevitable that all oracular trappings
such as witchcraft, the ephod, and the Urim and Thummim be
largely forgotten.

M. Pure Praise

"The floods have lifted up, O Jehovah, the floods have lifted
up their voice; the floods lift up their waves. Above the voices
of many waters, the mighty breakers of the sea, Jehovah on
high is mighty" (Ps. 93:3, 4).

This familiar Psalm comes very close to being pure praise,
free from petition expressed or implied. Occasionally such
prayers break into the Apocrypha and Pseudepigrapha: "Why
sleepest thou, O my soul, and blessest not the Lord? Sing a
new song unto God, who is worthy to be praised. Sing and be
wakeful against his awaking, for good is a psalm sung to God
from a glad heart" (Ps. Sol. 3:1, 2; cf. Sir. 39:14–16).

But most of the prayers of pure praise that occur in the
Apocrypha and Pseudepigrapha are found in the apocalypses
and are attributed to celestial beings. The sun and the moon
"give thanks and praise, and rest not, for unto them is their
thanksgiving rest" (I En. 41:7). Men on Mount Zion, the New
Jerusalem, praise the Lord with songs (IV Ezra 2:42), and the
cherubim and seraphim sing before the Lord, "Holy, holy, holy,
Lord Ruler of Sabaoth; heavens and earth are full of thy glory"
(II En. A 21:1). Similar celestial praises run through the New
Testament Apocalypse, where the six-winged creatures chant:
"Holy, holy, holy is the Lord God, the Almighty, who was, and
who is, and who is to come" (Rev. 4:8; see also Rev. 4:11;
5:13; 7:10, 12).

The outstanding instance of pure praise in the early rabbinic prayers is the Yotzer, or "Creator," the first of the two benedictions that precede the "Hear, O Israel": "Blessed art thou, O Lord our God, King of the universe, who formest light and createst darkness; who makest peace and createst all things; who givest light in mercy to the earth and to those who live thereon, and in goodness renewest every day the work of creation. Be thou blessed, O Lord our God, for the excellency of the work of thy hands and for the bright luminaries which thou hast made; let them glorify thee. Selah. Blessed art thou, O Lord, who formest the luminaries."

Such praise comes only from the mind which is able, at least for one elated moment, to conceive of God as being so tremendously and overwhelmingly great that all save his greatness is lost sight of, even the man's own need. It is no accident that the authors of apocalypse assign this sort of prayer to the celestials. What other content could occupy minds that are beyond need? Whoever prays this prayer has a foretaste of the only conceivable trait of a conscious immortality in God's presence.

But another prayer of quite different form is essentially the same. Instead of flowing from a moment of elation, it rises from a depth which would be despair if there were no faith. This is the prayer of absolute renunciation. "My Father," prayed Jesus in Gethsemane, "if it be possible, let this cup pass away from me: nevertheless, not as I will, but as thou wilt" (Mt. 26:39; see also Jn. 12:27, 28). This is to honor God not from a mountain of transfiguration, but from the valley of the shadow of death. No one can offer higher tribute to God's accepted sovereignty.

II. MEANS OF INDUCING GOD TO HEED
THE PRAYERS

A. AN APPEAL TO GOD'S DIGNITY OR PRIDE

Thus far we have considered how the aims of intertestamental prayers reveal the Jewish concept of God. Now we turn to the ways in which the Jews tried to induce God to answer their prayers, and to the light which these inducements throw upon intertestamental theology.

A natural transition is furnished by those prayers which honor God by attributing to him the quality which would best enable him to fulfil the aim of the petition. Such prayers contain an appeal to God's sense of dignity: that he demonstrate his possession of the quality.

This practice in prayer is very natural. The Old Testamental Psalmist, for instance, honored God by calling him Shepherd of Israel, then asked him to save Israel (Ps. 80). So also in the Apocryphal Book of Tobit, Raguel, Sarah's father, praised God for his previous mercy and asked him to show further mercy on Tobias and the bride (Tob. 8:17); and Sirach, praising God for proneness to forgive, urges all men to pray for forgiveness (Sir. 17:25, 29). "It is because of us sinners that you are called merciful," reasoned the author of Fourth Ezra; that is, if God was to retain the name, he should continue showing mercy to sinners (IV Ezra 8:31, 32). Angels attributed omniscience to God, then asked him to solve their problem as to what to do with the evil giants (I En. 9:4–11); Susanna, extolling God as one who knows all, implied that he should make this knowledge evident by vindicating her innocence at a time when no one but God and her accusers knew of it (Sus. 42, 43); and Wisdom, "the artificer of all things," was attributed to God in a prayer for enlightenment (Wisd. 7:15–22; see also II Bar. 21:12–18; 38:1–4; 54:1–6). Judith asked God to enable her, a woman, to rout

38

Assyria, for, she said, "thou art a God of the afflicted, thou art a helper of the oppressed, an upholder of the weak, a protector of the forlorn, a savior of them that are without hope" (Judith 9:9–11); but "the Hater of insolence," in the prayer of Eleazar, was the logical title for him who was to save the persecuted Jews from the proud Ptolemy (III Mac. 6:9); while to the grateful Jews themselves God was Savior and the Deliverer of Israel (III Mac. 6:29; 7:23). Judas's army called God "the Sovereign who crusheth forcibly the strength of his enemies," and asked him to grant victory in the storming of a walled city (II Mac. 12:28); but the priests, when praying that the temple be kept undefiled, addressed the "holy Lord, from whom is all hallowing" (II Mac. 14:34–36). "Lord of life and spirit" was the name Razis gave God when he pleaded for life in the day of resurrection (II Mac. 14:46). Daniel's prayer for the restoration of the captives, who were far away from Zion, hailed God as "Lord of all,...who rulest the world;" by influencing Babylon, he could vindicate his right to the honor bestowed upon him (As. Mos. 4:1–4).

The rabbinic prayer which follows the "Hear, O Israel" illustrates this type of inducement at a high level of dignity: "True and constant, established and enduring,...our Liberator and our Deliverer from everlasting,...arise to the help of Israel."

In all these prayers, which afford a logical transition from the study of aims to the study of inducements, the aim dictates the phrasing of the act of adoration by which the petitioner hopes to influence God to grant the request; and the phrasing of the act of adoration, in turn, contributes toward the petitioner's concept of God.

Almost all acts of adoration appeal to God's sense of his own dignity, sometimes at a lofty level, sometimes at a lower one. Among the latter, occasionally a prayer of the intertestamental period tries to evoke God's jealousy, a quality reminiscent of very ancient times when the Hebrews thought of God as having many stalwart divine rivals just beyond the boundaries of his little earthly range. For instance, as the Assyrian approached Palestine, the people of Jerusalem prayed that God not permit the city to be plundered and the sanctuary to be profaned to the delight of the gentiles (Judith 4:12). Again: "Let not the men whose thoughts are vanity," prayed Eleazar, "bless their vain gods for the destruction of thy beloved, saying, 'Neither has their God delivered them'" (III Mac. 6:11). Baruch reminds God that, after carrying the Jews into captivity, the enemy will boast at the shrines of their idols; "and what," he asks, "wilt thou do for thy great name?" (II Bar. 5:1). Most striking of all is the prayer of Esther, who reminds God that the enemy are trying to "open the mouth of the nations to give praise to vain idols" in order that "a king of flesh should be magnified for ever. Surrender not, O Lord, thy sceptre unto them that be not gods" (Add. Esth. 14:10, 11). Though monotheism is clearly established, prayers of this sort assume that God is still susceptible of the old jealousy.

Other prayers of the Apocrypha and Pseudepigrapha attempt to deal with God as if he felt a pride in his unique position as sole God. Sirach goads him: Let the alien peoples "see thy power . . . that they may know . . . that there is none other God but thee" (Sir. 36:3–5). Azariah's prayer includes virtually the same words, and adds, "Give glory to thy name, O Lord" (P. Azar. 20–22); while Judith urges God to let all nations know that he is God, "the God of all power and might" (Judith 9:14; see also II Mac. 1:27). Simon pleads for defense of the temple, lest Ptolemy boast: "We have trodden down the house of the sanctuary as the houses of the abominations are trodden down" (III Mac. 2:18); and, finally, Baruch attempts to strike the chord of God's pride by warning him that evil-doers may interpret his long-suffering as a sign of weakness (II Bar. 21:21).

Most of the numerous acts of adoration in intertestamental prayers, however, are simply spontaneous outbursts, proclaiming God's greatness and man's gratitude to him. From a study of the titles assigned to God, much can be learned about the Jews' understanding of God's nature.[15] Outstanding among these prayers of praise and thanksgiving is the Song of the Three Children, in which all creation hails God's enduring mercy. The obvious assumption is that God is gratified by praises; in

[15] Ralph Marcus, *Divine Names and Attributes in Hellenistic Jewish Literature*.

fact, this assumption comes to the surface not infrequently, as, for instance, when both Mordecai and Esther, in pleading for God's protection of the lives of the Jews, say to the Lord, "Destroy not the mouth of them that praise thee" (Add. Esth. 13:17; 14:9). One of the seven martyred brothers tells Antiochus that God will speedily punish him, "for thou cuttest out the tongue that sang songs of praise" unto God (IV Mac. 10:21). Baruch asks God who will praise him if Jerusalem is destroyed (I Bar. 2:17; II Bar. 3:5, 6; cf. Sir. 17:27). The Jews naturally felt that praises were the more acceptable if uttered "in the language of their fathers"— that is, in Hebrew, the language of holy writ, rather than in the vernacular Aramaic (II Mac. 15:29).

Praise, or benediction, is the dominant note of many early rabbinic prayers, and a doxology closes each of the prayers used in the ancient synagogue liturgy. "Blessed art thou" comes from pious Jewish lips as a familiar refrain. The rabbi ended his teaching with the Sanctification: "May his great name be blessed forever and to all eternity," and a prayer which grew out of this formula was inserted at the close of various portions of the synagogue service: "Magnified and hallowed be his great name." It was of course from this that Jesus took his "Hallowed be thy name" (Mt. 6:9), which constitutes the act of adoration in the Lord's Prayer.

The appeal to God's pride thus runs the long gamut from an evoking of jealousy to an evoking of God's rightful sense of his own infinite greatness.

B. AN APPEAL TO GOD'S LOVE OF THE BEAUTIFUL

Sirach's magnificent description of the temple ritual (Sir. 50:5–21) rises far above the primitive notion that offering, festival, tithe, hymn, and incense are ways of purchasing God's favor. Sacrifice is not a bribe (Sir. 35:12); the solemn rituals stir God's love of the beautiful as they stir Sirach's own esthetic response. Sirach therefore advocates sacrifice, always from one's own property, as a bulwark of prayer (Sir. 34:20–26; 46:16–18; see also II Mac. 3:31–35; 12:41–45; Judith 4:14, 15; Jub. 13:7–9;

13:16; T. Iss. 5:3; Sib. III, 624–628; V, 266–268). Certain of the sacrifices were part of a great sacred feast at which God, the honored though unseen guest, was especially inclined to heed petitions or accept the tribute of praise; so Enoch's son, after the great man's miraculous translation, sacrificed oxen and celebrated a three-day feast, praising God (II En. 68:5–7; cf. Jub. 16:25, 26), Likewise hymns, choruses, and instrumental music served to second important prayers, especially prayers of joy and thanksgiving. David is credited with establishing the custom at seasonal festivals (Sir. 47:8–10; see also I Mac. 4:24, 33; II Mac. 10:38; III Mac. 6:35; T. Jos. 8:5; Sib. III, 726; IV Ezra 2:42). The ceremonial trumpets blared as the people prostrated themselves for a prayer of lament or of earnest entreaty (I Mac. 4:39, 40; 5:31–33; Sir. 50:16, 17). The people carried palm branches as they voiced thanks to God (II Mac. 10:7); and they made procession to the temple to offer supplication (Sib. III, 716–718). In the symbolism of ritual, incense was said to carry prayers to heaven; so a sage spoke of "prayer and the propitiation of incense" (Wisd. 18:21; see also Lk. 1:9, 10). The Jew believed that all these ancient ceremonies roused in God the same esthetic response that the people themselves felt. Sirach, writing his fiftieth chapter, may well have imagined he was watching the temple ritual from God's point of view.

The liturgy of the synagogues has maintained something of this pageantry, and the early Christian advocated the doctrine of Christ's function as the high priest who continually offers sacrifice (Heb. 5:1–6); John's Apocalypse perpetuated the belief that incense, rising toward heaven, helped the supplications of the faithful (Rev. 8:3, 4); while later "the sacrifice of the mass" once more brought to the altar a pomp kindred to that which Israel believed could turn God's ear toward prayer.

C. The Appeal to God's Bargaining Instinct

The section on prayers for aid in warfare[16] opens with Jephthah's rash vow to sacrifice whatever came out of his house to meet him, provided he was victorious against his foes (Judg.

---

[16] See I, A above.

11:30, 31; see also Gen. 28:20–22). This custom of bargaining with God as if he were a merchant in the bazaar, survived in mellowed form throughout the intertestamental period; in fact, it still has a place in Judaism and Christianity.

Though the first living creature to meet Jephthah was his daughter, he could no more alter his vow than could a slinger recall his missile. The word had been spoken and God had granted victory over the Ammonites: Jephthah had to sacrifice his daughter. So Sirach says: "Delay not to pay thy vow in due time . . . . Before thou vowest, prepare thy vows, and be not as one that tempteth God" (Sir. 18:22, 23).

When Holofernes appeared on the boundary of Palestine, all Jerusalem prayed, and the priests offered up the vows of the people (Judith 4:14). Before joining battle with the Syrian general Lysias, Judas and his men uttered a prayer which was climaxed by a vow of hymns as payment for victory (I Mac. 4:33). The Syrian king Antiochus, smitten with a loathsome disease which made the flesh fall from his body, sought healing from Jehovah by a vow to free the holy city, to make the Jews equal to the citizens of Athens, to restore and support the temple, and himself to become a Jew (II Mac. 9:13–17). It is noteworthy, however, that the bargaining prayers of the Apocrypha and Pseudepigrapha can be counted on the fingers of one hand.

Sometimes the vow, instead of being used as an inducement for the fulfilling of a petition, became a means of adding force to a prayer of thanksgiving. For instance, Heliodorus, when, in answer to the high priest's prayer, God had restored him to health, "vowed very great vows to him who had preserved his life" (II Mac. 3:35).

The Mishnah, a written record of oral tradition concerning the Jewish Law (c. A. D. 200), contains numerous minute regulations about vows (e. g., Hallah 1:2), and, as Paul's shearing of his hair indicates, Christians also used vows (Acts 18:18; cf. Acts 21:23, 24). But it is important to bear in mind the fact that vows pledging highly ethical action and vows seconding prayers of thanksgiving are far above the level of a mercenary bargain with God. The latter are often no bargain at all, and the former imply that God delights in man's righteous actions.

D. THE ACT OF GOING TO OR FACING A PLACE
OF THE SPECIAL PRESENCE OF GOD

"And Samuel said, 'Gather all Israel to Mizpah, and I will pray for you unto Jehovah' " (I Sam. 7:5). Nine centuries later, Judas Maccabeus and his followers "gathered themselves together and came to Mizpah, over against Jerusalem; for in Mizpah there had been aforetime a place of prayer for Israel" (I Mac. 3:46).

Hebron also was a place where God seemed especially near. It was at this place that Abraham entertained angels; here stood his altar; here he and Isaac and Jacob were buried; and here David was anointed. Therefore a Pseudepigraphic writer of the first century A. D., using the name of Baruch, chose this as his place of divine revelation, where the word was spoken to him in reponse to his prayers and fasting (II Bar. 47:1, 2).

Third Maccabees relates how the Jews who had escaped from Egypt after Ptolemy Philopator's persecutions, held a festival n•honor of a safe journey homeward and "dedicated a place of prayer on the spot where they had held their festival" (III Mac. 7:20). Evidently they had felt an unusual degree of God's presence at their festival.

But of course the temple was the place of places for God's indwelling. The words which Solomon is said to have spoken at the dedication of the sanctuary express with eloquence the conflict between a theoretic belief in God's omnipresence and the practical belief in his special presence within the holy precinct: "Will God in very deed dwell on the earth? Behold, heaven and the heaven of heavens cannot contain thee; how much less this house that I have builded! Yet have thou respect unto the prayer of thy servant, and to his supplication, O Jehovah my God, to hearken unto the cry and to the prayer which thy servant prayeth before thee this day; that thine eyes may be open toward this house night and day, even toward the place whereof thou hast said, 'My name shall be there'; to hearken unto the prayer which thy servant shall pray toward this place. And hearken thou to the supplication of thy servant, and of thy people Israel, when they shall pray toward this place:

yea, hear thou in heaven, thy dwelling-place; and when thou hearest, forgive" (I K. 8:27–30).

Therefore it was in front of the temple that the people prostrated themselves and fasted as they prayed for protection from Holofernes (Judith 4:9–15), just as priests, maidens, mothers, and nurses had rushed there in confusion to raise supplication when Ptolemy Philopator had threatened the Holy of Holies (III Mac. 1:20–24), only to be struck down in response to the high priest's prayer before the holy place (III Mac. 2:1–22); for, said the priest in his petition, "loving the house of Israel thou didst promise that if . . . we should come to this place and make our supplication, thou wouldst hear our prayer" (III Mac. 2:10). The priestly prayer which brought Heliodorus to the brink of death was spoken in anguish before the altar (II Mac. 3:15); and Judas's band prayed at the same step (II Mac. 10:25, 26). After Titus had destroyed the temple, the writer using Baruch's name described how the prophet went to the ruins of the Holy of Holies and sat down to pray for a message to give his despairing people when the first of the temples had been torn down (II Bar. 34:1—35:5). The author of the Life of Adam and Eve, since the geographic location of his story precluded his referring to Palestinian praying-places, attributed to Adam's sons a "house of prayer, where they used to worship the Lord God" (L. A. E. 30:2); but on other occasions they prayed at the gates of the garden, in the hope that God was listening from beyond the wall (L. A. E. 31:1; 36:1, 2).

When it was impossible for the Jew to go to an ancient praying-place or to the temple, he tried to carry on the tradition by merely facing Jerusalem for his prayers. Just as Daniel prayed by windows opening toward Jerusalem (Dan. 6:10), so Zerubbabel, according to an Apocryphal author of the Maccabean period, "lifted his face to heaven toward Jerusalem" as he praised God for the opportunity to rebuild the temple (I Esd. 4:58; cf. Tob. 3:11, 12).

The Mishnah stipulates concerning the man who wants to say the Eighteen Benedictions: "If he is riding on an ass, he should dismount. If he cannot dismount, he should turn his face (toward Jerusalem); and if he cannot turn his face, he should direct his heart toward the Holy of Holies" (Mish. Ber. 4:5). It was customary for the leader who read the prayers in the synagogue to face the ark in which was kept the scroll of the Law, and this ark in turn rested in a niche of the wall that faced Jerusalem.

Though Jesus revered the temple, he insisted that men should confine their worship of God neither to Jerusalem nor to the mountain held sacred by the Samaritans, since God is spiritual and omnipresent (Jn. 4:19–24). Warning against ostentatious prayer in the synagogues or on street corners, he advocated the use of one's inner chamber (Mt. 6:5, 6) and would doubtless have approved of the disciples' upper room (Acts 1:13, 14). His own custom was to climb some lonely hill (Mt. 14:23; Lk. 6:12; 9:28) and withdraw from his most intimate comrades (Lk. 22:41; cf. Acts 9:40). To Jesus the place was of little importance, save as it offered seclusion. But the old Jewish belief concerning God's special presence at the altar was destined to reassert itself in the Christian church in a new form. Evidently it is hard not to localize God.

E. A Reminder of Past Promises or of Precedent

"Remember Abraham, Isaac, and Israel, thy servants to whom thou swarest by thine own self and saidst unto them, 'I will multiply your seed as the stars of heaven, and all this land that I have spoken of will I give unto your seed, and they shall inherit it for ever' " (Ex. 32:13).

The inducement which the Jews employed most regularly in their prayers was a reminder of God's past promises. Again and again the petitions of the Apocrypha and Pseudepigrapha call on God to remember the covenant he made with the ancient patriarchs (I Mac. 4:10; II Mac. 8:14, 15; P. Azar. 11–13; As. Mos. 4:1, 2; 11:17; IV Ezra 4:22, 23; Ps. Sol. 9:16–19; 12:7), to remember that the land is the inheritance of the Jews (Judith 9:12; Sir. 36:11), that he is their God (Ps. Sol. 8:37), and that they are his chosen people (II Mac. 1:24–26; 14:15; Judith 12:8; I Bar. 2:11; Add. Esth. 13:15; Jub. 1:17; II Bar. 48:20), his slaves (II Mac. 8:29), and his inheritance (Judith 13:5; Add. Esth. 14:5; Jub. 1:19; IV Ezra 8:15, 16; Ps. Sol. 7:2), sanctified to him (Judith 6:19), and known by his name (II Mac. 8:15; IV Ezra 4:25). The author of the Life of Adam and Eve represents Adam as praising God for his promise that Adam's seed would forever have the right to serve God (L. A. E. 27:3—28:1), Baruch recalls to God's mind the promises made to the great lawgiver (II Bar. 3:9), and the Psalmist entreats God to make good the pledge that the sceptre would ever remain with David's seed (Ps. Sol. 17:5, 23).

Closely allied to these reminders of God's promises is the appeal to precedent in God's past relations with his people. Judas, for instance, prayed: "Blessed art thou, O Savior of Israel, who . . . didst deliver the army of the Philistines into the hands of Jonathan . . . . Shut up this army in the hands of thy people Israel" (I Mac. 4:30, 31). He also pleaded that, just as God had punished Sennacherib's blasphemy by sending an angel to strike down 185,000 of the Assyrians, so he would punish the blasphemous Nicanor by sending an angel to carry terror before the Jews (I Mac. 7:41, 42; II Mac. 15:22, 23; cf. III Mac. 2:1–20); and that he would help the Jews take Caspin, a walled city, even as he had helped Joshua's men take the walled city of Jericho (II Mac. 12:15). Judith's prayer was that God use a woman's deceit to overthrow Holofernes as he had used a woman's dishonor to bring about the fall of the princes of Shechem (Judith 9:2–14), and Baruch asked Jerusalem to pray that God would grant the captives in Babylon (symbolic of the Seleucid Empire) favor in the eyes of their masters, just as he had performed wonders to bring his people out of Egypt (I Bar. 2:11–15). God was thus he who always upheld his people by manifesting himself (II Mac. 14:15).

The suggestion of the covenant is a commonplace in the early rabbinic prayers: "O Rock of Israel, arise to the help of Israel, and deliver, according to thy promise, Judah and Israel" (Geul.). "Blessed art thou, O Lord, that guardest thy people Israel forever" (Hashkibenu. Cf. Ben. XIX). "Thou hast chosen us" (Ahab.).

In the gospels and epistles the ancient covenant is renewed

through Christ. Zacharias, the father of John the Baptist, thanks God for remembering "his holy covenant: the oath which he sware unto Abraham our father, to grant unto us that we, being delivered out of the hand of our enemies, should serve him without fear in holiness and righteousness before him all our days" (Lk. 1:72–75).

In this appeal based on a reminder of a promise to be kept or a precedent to be maintained, the prayers point toward a concept of God as one who is "true and constant, established and enduring" (Geul.). Here is the seed of a belief that God rules nature and men's lives in a way which is not capricious, but orderly. His will is law "as it was in the beginning, is now, and ever shall be."

F. Various Ways of Appealing to God's Justice

"And when ye spread forth your hands, I will hide mine eyes from you; yea, when ye make many prayers, I will not hear; your hands are full of blood" (Is. 1:15).

"Jehovah is far from the wicked, but he heareth the prayer of the righteous" (Prov. 15:29).

This principle, well established by the Old Testament prophets, dominates many prayers of the Apocrypha and Pseudepigrapha. "Better is prayer with truth," explained the angel Raphael (Tob. 12:8). One of the seventy-two Jewish scholars told Ptolemy to emulate God, by whom "the petitions of the worthy are always fulfilled" (Arist. 191, 192; see also Sir. 15:9, 10; Arist. 17, 18, 193; I En. 97:5; Sib. III, 716–719; Ps. Sol. 6:8, 9). And the sage Ahikar warned God that unless the righteous man's prayer was answered, men would conclude that goodness and devotion to God are of no avail (Ahik., Syr. A 1:4, 5). The plea of either righteous conduct or piety was advanced by Sarah, Tobias's bride-to-be (Tob. 3:14), by Tobias himself (Tob. 8:7), by Judith for her people (Judith 8:17–19), by Daniel (Bel 38), by Esther (Add. Esth. 14:15–18), by Solomon (Ps. Sol. 1:1, 2), by Hezekiah (Sir. 48:20–22; see also II Bar. 63:3–5), and by Baruch (II Bar. 38:1–4). God is moved by the words of the upright.

Conversely, the prayer of Eve, who had twice fallen before the wiles of the tempter, was not heard (L. A. E. 19:2), and similarly, prayers directed against wicked men were thought to make strong appeal to God: for instance, the prayer against blasphemous Nicanor (I Mac. 7:38) and that against the persecutor Antiochus (II Mac. 8:4). On one occasion, just before a critical battle against the Syrians, the Jews unrolled the scroll of the Law before Jehovah as they prayed (I Mac. 3:48), "in order that the roll of the Law might bear witness before God against the blasphemous proceeding of the gentiles."[17]

Sometimes the law-observance which was supposed to appeal to God's sense of justice was merely a matter of ritual, such as ablution prior to the prayer. Judith bathed in the captured spring before praying for success in her hazardous mission (Judith 12:7, 8); the seventy-two scholars washed their hands in the sea each morning before praying for guidance in their task of translating the Law (Arist. 305, 306); and the Sibyl urged even the gentiles to wash their whole bodies in ever running rivers before praying (Sib. IV, 162–166) — though the usual purpose of this practice was to free Jews from the contagion of contacts with outsiders.

In other prayers, the petitioner appealed to God's fairness by first doing his best, then asking God's help. For instance, one of the seventy-two translators suggested that Ptolemy, in order to be free from grief, live the sort of good life that normally does not invite grief, and pray for protection from unexpected ills (Arist. 232, 233). Judas's men won victory by "fighting with their hands while they prayed to God with their hearts" (II Mac. 15:27), and Sirach taught concerning artisans that their prayer is in the practice of their craft (Sir. 38:34, textual note). This all implies that God says, "You do your share, if you expect me to do mine."

Charity is a virtue especially marked as one which will induce God to heed prayer (Tob. 12:8–10). The man who is generous in alms has no reason to be discouraged about his prayers, says

---

[17] R. H. Charles, *The Apocrypha and Pseudepigrapha*, vol. I, p. 79, note on I Mac. 3:48.

Sirach (Sir. 7:10); just as the New Testament makes it clear that Cornelius's alms fortified his prayers (Acts 10:1–4).

Closely akin to charity is the spirit of forgiveness — another potent means of influencing God. "Forgive thy neighbor the injury done to thee, and then, when thou prayest, thy sins will be forgiven. Man cherisheth anger against another; and doth he seek healing from God? On a man like himself he hath no mercy; and doth he make supplication for his own sins?" (Sir. 28:2–4; cf. T. Jos. 18:2; Arist. 227.) God's justice could brook no such inconsistency in a man. Two centuries later, Jesus, through his model prayer, recommended the same reasonable way of gaining forgiveness by forgiving; for, he explained, "if ye forgive not men their trespasses, neither will your Father forgive your trespasses" (Mt. 6:15).

Some prayers rely not upon the merit of the petitioner, but upon that of the fathers long dead, in accordance with a belief in "the communion of the saints," through which merit is shared.[18] This is quite consistent with the Old Testament warning to the effect that the sins of the fathers are visited upon the children, even to the third and fourth generation (Ex. 20:5; Lam. 5:7), but is quite counter to the teaching of Ezekiel and Jeremiah to the effect that the proverbial sour grapes shall set on edge the teeth of him who eats them (Ezek. 18:2–4; Jer. 31:29, 30; cf. Dt. 24:16).

This clash of opinion continues through the intertestamental period and thereafter. Baruch advises: "Pray ... that the Mighty One may be reconciled to you and that he may not reckon the multitude of your sins, but remember the rectitude of your fathers" (II Bar. 84:10), and an early rabbinic prayer says, "for our fathers' sake, who trusted in thee and whom thou didst teach the statutes of life, be gracious unto us too, and teach us" (Ahab.). But at least one Apocryphal author eschews the privilege of dipping into the reservoir of merit: "We do not present our supplication before thee, O Lord our God, for the righteousness of our fathers and of our kings" (I Bar. 2:19), and John the Baptist denounces the belief that Abraham's

[18] Ralph Marcus, *Law in the Apocrypha*, pp. 14–16.

merit will aid the patriarch's descendants at the judgment (Mt. 3:8–10).

The doctrine of atonement through the death of martyrs is a reassertion of faith in God's recognition of the reservoir of merit. In the Old Testament, the Second Isaiah foreshadows the tenet, and, among the Apocrypha and Pseudepigrapha, Fourth Maccabees relates how Eleazar, being burned to death for refusing to eat unclean food at the command of Antiochus Epiphanes, "lifted his eyes to God and said, 'Thou, O God, knowest that though I might save myself I am dying by fiery torments for thy Law . . . . Be merciful unto thy people, and let our punishment be a satisfaction in their behalf. Make my blood their purification, and take my soul to ransom their souls' " (IV Mac. 6:27–29). The seventh of the martyred brothers offered a similar prayer concerning the efficacy of his own death (II Mac. 7:37, 38; IV Mac. 12:18), and one of the three men in the fiery furnace suggested to his two comrades that their deaths were sacrificial (IV Mac. 13:12). The parallel in early Christian belief is too obvious to need comment: God's justice permits the rank and file to ask God to remember the martyr's death, just as the martyr had a right to pray that his own death might be a propitiation for the shortcomings of many (see, for instance, Heb. 2:9).

The use of an intercessor is another way of appealing to God's justice, for the intercessor is always of superior moral rank; in fact, that is why intercession is considered effective.[19] Sometimes the intercessor is merely a righteous man; sometimes also a man of religious authority, that is, a prophet, priest, or scribe; occasionally he is the disembodied spirit of a religious leader; and with increasing frequency in the Apocrypha and Pseudepigrapha he is an angel.

The need for an interceding mediator came as a result of God's increasing distance or absoluteness. Isaiah, for instance, has God say, "My thoughts are not your thoughts, neither are your

[19] Philo goes a step farther by contending that the reason why the righteous man can intercede effectively is that he partakes of the divine Logos; and the Logos, who mediates between God and men, is the active power in all intercessory prayer. See Larson, "Prayer of Petiton in Philo," *Journal of Biblical Literature*, LXV (1946), 196–97.

ways my ways .... For as the heavens are higher than the earth, so are my ways higher than your ways, and my thoughts than your thoughts" (Is. 55:8, 9). Though Job concluded, "There is no umpire betwixt us [God and me] that might lay his hand upon us both" (Job 9:33), the Old Testament mentions numerous instances of the belief in intercessory mediation by men. Abraham prayed for Ishmael (Gen. 17:18), for Sodom (Gen. 18:23–33), and for Abimelech (Gen. 20:17); the prophet Moses interceded for his people (Ex. 32:11–13), as did Samuel (I Sam. 12:23); and Elijah prayed for the enlightenment of the people by a miracle (I K. 18:36, 37).

In the Apocrypha and Pseudepigrapha intercession by the righteous person is still a commonplace: for example, the despairing elders of Bethulia say to Judith, "Pray thou for us, because thou art a goodly woman" (Judith 8:31); Enoch urges all the devout to pray for the souls of others (II En. 61:1, 2); and Adam, who is morally superior to Eve, is successful in his intercession for Eve during her ordeal of childbirth (L. A. E. 20:2—21:3). Moreover the prayers of intercession by prophet, priest, or scribe are legion (II Bar. 85:1, 2): the fallen angels ask Enoch, the man of God, to write a prayer in their behalf and to present it to God (I En. 13:4; II En. A 7:4, 5); Levi the priest prays for all his scattered brethren (T. N. 6:7, 8); and the list of intercessors goes on to include Eleazar the priest (III Mac. 6:1–15), the priests of the temple at the time of Nicanor's threat (I Mac. 7:36–38), Onias the high priest (II Mac. 3:31), Moses, the greatest of prophets (As. Mos. 11:17), and Baruch and Jeremiah, whose prayers are "as a strong wall" to Jerusalem (II Bar. 2:1, 2). In the New Testament, Simon the sorcerer begs the apostle Peter to intercede for him (Acts 8:24), and James assures the sick that the prayers of righteous men, especially elders, will bring healing (Jas. 5:13–18).

According to those of the Jews who believed in life after death, great intercessors, even after death, might continue praying for others. Judas, in "a reliable dream, a sort of vision," saw the high priest Onias and the prophet Jeremiah — both long since dead — pleading with God in behalf of the Jewish community (II Mac. 15:11–16).

It is noteworthy that in the Old Testament the intercessor is always a man, never an angel, with rare exceptions in Zechariah 1:12 and in Daniel 12:1, a late passage. But in the Apocrypha and Pseudepigrapha the mediator who intercedes is usally an angel. Raphael explains to Tobit and Tobias that he is one of the seven angels who carry up the prayers of the saints and go into the presence of the glory of the Lord (Tob. 12:15). Michael, commander of these angels, not only "comes down to receive the prayers of men," but also gathers up from his subordinates all the deeds of men and shows these deeds to God (III Bar. 11:4—17:1). It is doubtless to Michael that Levi alludes in speaking of "the angel who intercedeth for the nation of Israel and for all the righteous" (T. L. 5:7). Instances of angelic intercession are strewn all the way from the beginning to the close of the intertestamental era (see also L. A. E. 9:3; S. L. A. E. 31:1; Apoc. Mos. 29:3–6; 33:5; I En. 9:3; 39:5; 40:3–10; 47:2–4; T. D. 6:2).

Only on the day of judgment is intercession banned. Enoch warned his sons not to say, "Our father is standing before God; he will stand forward for us on the day of judgment" (II En. 53:1). "At the end there will be no place for prayer . . . nor intercession of the fathers, nor prayer of the prophets, nor help of the righteous" (II Bar. 85:12; cf. IV Ezra 7:102–115).

The strong trend toward a belief in angelic intercession is not registered in early rabbinic prayers; it does not make itself felt in official Jewish prayers until the Middle Ages.[20]

But Christianity made the concept an integral part of orthodoxy. "Another angel came," wrote John of Patmos, "and stood over the altar, having a golden censer; and there was given unto him much incense, that he should add it unto the prayers of all the saints upon the golden altar which was before the throne. And the smoke of the incense, with the prayers of the saints, went up before God out of the angel's hand" (Rev. 8:3, 4). But it is, of course, the eternal Christ who stands before God as the chief intercessor according to the Christian faith (Rom. 8:33, 34). "Wherefore also he is able to save to the uttermost

---

[20] Felix Perles, "Prayers, Jewish," E. R. E., vol. X, p. 194.

them that draw near unto God through him, seeing he ever liveth to make intercession for them" (Heb. 7:25; see also Lk. 12:8, 9; Jn. 14:16). One of the paradoxes of Christianity lies here: that the Jesus who taught the "Our Father"— a prayer whose opening words draw God close to men — was destined to be considered also the divine intercessor between mankind and a strangely distant God.

To recapitulate: the petitioner could appeal to God's justice (1) by seconding his prayer with his own righteousness, especially charity, or (2) by dipping into the reservoir of merit of his fathers, of the martyrs, or of some superior intercessor, though in the minds of many Jews there was serious doubt as to whether a man could rely on any merit other than his own.

G. The Appeal to God's Mercy and Compassion

Repentance is normally the means by which the Jew appeals to God in a prayer for forgiveness. "I had heard of thee by the hearing of the ear," said Job; "but now mine eye seeth thee: wherefore I abhor myself and repent in dust and ashes" (Job 42:5, 6). Though the prayer of repentance implicitly or explicitly acknowledges God's justice, the primary appeal is to his mercy and compassion.

There is no better description of the penitential prayer than is given by Sirach: "Turn unto the Most High, and turn away from iniquity, and vehemently hate the abominable thing" (Sir. 17:26; see also Sir. 21:1). The essence of repentance is "a contrite heart and a humble spirit" (P. Azar. 16). The prayer usually includes some such confession as Manasses' words: "I am not worthy to behold and see the height of heaven by reason of the multitude of mine iniquities" (P. Man. 9), and the climax is the plea for pardon: "I humbly beseech thee, forgive me, O Lord, forgive me" (P. Man. 13). The intent to turn from the evil course is always implied or expressed (I Bar. 2:8; Sib. III, 624–631; IV, 163–166). A New Testament writer thus summarizes the efficacy of the *confiteor* as an appeal to God's mercy: "If we confess our sins, he is faithful and righteous to

forgive us our sins and to cleanse us from all unrighteousness"
(I Jn. 1:9).

Since, in response to repentance, God cleanses men from sin
(Ps. Sol. 9:12), and, staying his wrath (Sib. IV, 169), lifts the
penalty, repentance becomes a means of inducing God to allow
escape from all sorts of punitive evils, such as illness (Sir. 38:9,
10), the blight of being childless (T. Jud. 19:2), and the misery of
exile (I Bar. 2:12–14).

The usual way of demonstrating repentance was the wearing
of sackcloth, as at Nineveh, where even the beasts were covered
with the rags of penitence (Jon. 3:8). But the wearing of sackcloth was by no means confined to those who were praying for
forgiveness; the Jew resorted to the traditional garb of mourning
whenever he wanted to appeal to God's compassion in an urgent
entreaty (I Mac. 3:47–53; II Mac. 3:19–21; 10:25, 26; Judith
4:9–15; I Bar. 4:20; Add. Esth. 14:1–19). As in the act of
mourning, the petitioner often threw ashes, dust, or dung into
his hair (I Mac. 3:47; 4:39, 40; 11:71; II Mac. 10:25; Judith 4:11;
Add. Esth. 14:2; L. A. E. 31:1; 36:1), wailed and wept aloud
(I Mac. 4:39, 40; II Mac. 11:6; 13:12; III Mac. 1:16; 5:6, 7,
25, 50, 51; 6:14, 17; Judith 7:29; I Bar. 1:5; L. A. E. 4:3; 31:1;
36:1; Apoc. Mos. 42:8; T. Jos. 8:1; As. Mos. 3:8, 9; II Bar. 35:1;
III Bar. 1:1, 2; IV Ezra 5:20), smote his breast (Apoc. Mos.
42:8), and tore his garments (I Mac. 3:47; 4:39; 11:71). In order
to move God to pity, Adam stood in the Jordan up to his neck
for forty days and, feeling that Eve could not endure such hard-
ship, allowed her to stand likewise in the Tigris for thirty-seven
days (L. A. E. 6:1, 2).

The sackcloth and ashes passed over into the teachings of
Jesus. "Then he began to upbraid the cities wherein most of
his mighty works were done, because they repented not: 'Woe
unto thee, Chorazin! Woe unto thee, Bethsaida! For if the
mighty works had been done in Tyre and Sidon which were done
in you, they would have repented long ago in sackcloth and
ashes' " (Mt. 11:20, 21). Furthermore, the author of Hebrews
refers to Jesus as offering up prayers "with strong crying and
tears" (Heb. 5:7).

From early times the Hebrews had used fasting as a way of

stirring God's compassion when they were urgent in their prayer.[21] For instance, when Bathsheba's first child was stricken, David fasted as long as there was any hope for the infant's recovery (II Sam. 12:22, 23). Petitioners in the Apocrypha and Pseudepigrapha continue to utilize the fast to support pressing pleas for everything from forgiveness to the gift of a revelation (I Mac. 3:46, 47; II Mac. 13:10–12; Sir. 34:26; I Bar. 1:5; T. Jos. 3:3, 4; Ahik., Arm. 2:49). The usual length of the fast seems to have been seven days (II Bar. 47:2; IV Ezra 5:20; 6:35). On two occasions Ezra fasted for seven days by confining his diet to wild plants of the field (IV Ezra 9:26–28; 12:51).

The Mishnah gives directions for fasting in connection with prayers for rain (Mish. Taanith 1), and the Christians at Antioch "fasted and prayed and laid their hands on" Barnabas and Saul before sending them out as itinerant teachers (Acts 13:3; see also Acts 14:23).

Another way of evoking God's compassion is sexual abstinence. Reminiscent of Ecclesiastes 3:5 is Naphtali's advice to his sons: "There is a season for a man to embrace his wife, and a season to abstain therefrom for his prayer" (T. N. 8:8). Paul also advocates this custom of abstinence for prayer, but with caution (I Cor. 7:5).

The Jewish prayer-postures not only impressed the devotee with the sanctity of prayer, but also appealed to God's mercy through a suggestion of a man's self-abasement, respect, or earnestness. According to the Old Testament, Abraham stood when he prayed for Sodom (Gen. 18:22), Solomon knelt during the dedication-prayer for the temple (I K. 8:54), the wanderers in the wilderness fell on their faces as they pleaded for relief from a deadly plague (Num. 16:45), and Elijah, in praying for rain, "bowed himself down upon the earth, and put his face between his knees" (I K. 18:42). Except during prostration, the petitioner often raised his hands (Ps. 63:4) or spread them forth to heaven (Ex. 9:29; I K. 8:54; Is. 1:15), as if to receive a gift.

The Apocrypha and Pseudepigrapha sometimes describe the posture of prayer as a bowing of the knees, bowing down, or

---

[21] This was not the only function of the fast; sometimes fasting was a mark of mourning, and frequently it became an outward sign of penitence.

kneeling (II Mac. 2:1; Judith 13:17; L. A. E. 50:3; As. Mos. 4:1), and sometimes as prostration, presumably on the knees, with face and arms on the ground (I Mac. 4:39, 40, 55; II Mac. 3:15; 10:4, 25, 26; 13:10–12; III Mac. 1:16; 5:50, 51; Judith 4:11; 6:18; 9:1; Sir. 50:17; L. A. E. 31:1; 36:1, 2; T. Jos. 4:3; Sib. III, 716, 717). As in the Old Testament, except in prostration the hands may be raised to heaven (II Mac. 3:15; III Mac. 5:25; Sib. IV, 166) or spread out (II Mac. 15:21; III Mac. 2:1; Sir. 48:20; 51:19; L. A. E. 50:3; As. Mos. 4:1), and naturally the face looks upward (Sus. 35; Apoc. Mos. 42:8; IV Mac. 6:26).

It is interesting to note that the Eighteen Benedictions are often referred to as the Amidah, which means "standing," for that is the proper posture during these prayers (Mish. Ber. 4:5; cf. Lk. 18:11), though for others of the rabbinic prayers the people bowed the head or knelt.[22] The School of Shammai said: "In the evening all should recline when they recite (the 'Hear, O Israel'), but in the morning they should stand up, for it is written, 'And when thou liest down and when thou risest up' " (Mish. Ber. 1:3). But the School of Hillel perceived that the author of Deuteronomy was referring to hours, not to postures.

Jesus and the early Christians retained the Jewish custom of standing during prayer (Mk. 11:25; Lk. 18:13) or kneeling (Lk. 22:41; Acts 9:40; 20:36; 21:5; Eph. 3:14) or prostrating themselves (Mt. 26:39; Mk. 14:35). Unless prostrate, they sometimes raised their hands (I Tim. 2:8) and looked upward to the Father of mercies (Mt. 14:19; Jn. 11:41).

Yet another appeal to God's compassion rather than to his sense of justice was the act of the congregation's uniting in prayer. On occasion the group united only in the Amen, just as Sarah said Amen with Tobias after his prayer on the wedding night (Tob. 8:8), but more frequently in the Apocrypha and Pseudepigrapha the throng joins in the actual supplication, crying to God in concert (II Mac. 3:20; III Mac. 1:23; Judith 4:12; Sus. 60; Add. Esth. 13:18). This union in prayer reaches poetic expression in the Slavonic Life of Adam and Eve: "The angels came together and all living creatures, wild and tame, and all

22 Felix Perles, "Prayers, Jewish," E. R. E., vol. X, p. 194.

birds that fly, and they surrounded Adam like a wall, praying to God for Adam" (S. L. A. E. 37:1). Probably the most familiar instance in poetic form is the Song of the Three Children, where all creation unites in praising and exalting God.

As for the early rabbinic prayers, each of the Eighteen Benedictions, recited by a leader in the synagogue, ended with an Amen from the congregation, and the congregation's Amen followed each sentence of the Priestly Blessing.[23]

Jesus taught: "If two of you shall agree on earth as touching anything that they shall ask, it shall be done for them of my Father who is in heaven" (Mt. 18:19; see also Acts 1:14), and Paul mentioned the congregation's responding with an Amen (I Cor. 14:15, 16; see also Rev. 19:4). Probably the original feeling was that God is more strongly influenced by concerted prayer than by an individual's plea.

From Old Testament times the Hebrew had been convinced that no attitude appealed to God's compassion more than did humility. " 'Because thy heart was tender and thou didst humble thyself before Jehovah,' " said the prophetess to King Josiah, " '. . . I also have heard thee,' saith Jehovah" (II K. 22:19). The appeal of humility flows through many prayers of the intertestamental period. The Bethulians, for instance, contrast the arrogance of Holofernes with their own abasement (Judith 6:18, 19), and Judith prays to the God of the lowly (Judith 9:11). It is the appeal of humility that brings God's favor to Joseph's prayer (T. Jos. 10:2), and both Mordecai and Esther, seeking answer to their entreaties, are careful to remind God that they are not guilty of any arrogance (Add. Esth. 13:12; 14:15, 16). One sure way to induce God to heed a prayer against a foe is to call his attention to their consuming pride (II Mac. 1:28; III Mac. 5:13; II Bar. 63:4). Since humility usually characterizes the poor, Sirach says that the prayer of a poor man reaches God's ears (Sir. 21:5; cf. Sir. 35:13; Ps. Sol. 18:3), and Joseph, avoiding ostentation in his piety, was careful to go to his chamber to pray (T. Jos. 3:3), as Jesus later advised his disciples to do (Mt. 6:5, 6). The classic early Christian illustra-

[23] W. O. E. Oesterley, *Jewish Background of the Christian Liturgy*, p. 71.

tion of the efficacy of the prayer from humble lips is the parable of the Pharisee and the publican in the temple (Lk. 18:10–14).

Earnestness is another trait that commends prayer to God's compassion. There is no need to mention the frequency with which the reader senses this quality in the Old Testament Psalms. The author of the Wisdom of Solomon prays with all his heart (Wisd. 8:21), and Baruch advocates the same spirit in supplication (II Bar. 84:10; cf. Judith 4:9). On this point the Mishnah is explicit, as usual: "None may stand up to say the Tefillah (the Eighteen Benedictions) save in sober mood. The pious men of old used to wait an hour before they said the Tefillah, that they might direct their heart toward God" (Mish. Ber. 5:1). And conversely: "He that makes his prayer a fixed task, his prayer is no supplication" (Mish. Ber. 4:4). Earnestness characterized also the early Christian approach to God (Acts 12:5), but Christians usually defined the most essential attitude as one of faith rather than of earnestness (Mt. 21:22; Jas. 1:6).

A belief which is a commonplace in the Apocrypha and Pseudepigrapha but is not prevalent in the Old Testament is that importunity in prayer evokes the mercy of God. Doubtless, insistent praying was practiced in Old Testament times, as, for instance, by Elijah on Mount Carmel (I K. 18:42–44), but the record contains few examples of such praying. Daniel's three prayers daily must be dated at the very end of the Old Testament period, and even in this custom we have no hint of importunity — only of fidelity and of courage under the danger of persecution (Dan. 6:10).

The belief that prayer should be importunate is based on the assumption that, if ungracious men yield to insistent petition just to avoid the bother of hearing it repeated further, surely God in his mercy will be influenced by the continual prayers of those for whose welfare he is already deeply concerned. The attitude of insistence goes far beyond mere patience in praying, such as Sirach and the Psalmist advocate (Sir. 7:10; Ps. Sol. 2:40), and such as Joseph is reputed to have practiced (T. Jos. 10:1, 2). God was thought to be gratified over faithful daily prayer (As. Mos. 11:11; Ps. Sol. 6:1, 6, 7), especially prayer before dawn (Wisd. 16:27, 28; T. Jos. 3:6). But God's compassion was profoundly stirred by an importunate petition that lasted all night (Judith 6:21), or from noon through the night (T. Jos. 8:1), or three days (II Mac. 13:12; Add. Esth. 15:4), or many days (Arist. 316), or fifteen days (S. L. A. E. 31:1), or every hour day and night (As. Mos. 11:17), or hourly and daily for thirty years (IV Ezra 9:44).

There is no evidence of such importunity in the early rabbinic prayers. The Mishnah gives definite regulations concerning reciting the "Hear, O Israel" with its proper prayers twice daily and concerning the saying of certain portions of the Eighteen Benedictions three times daily (Mish. Ber. 1:1, 2; 4:1), but all these practices are only pious duty, not importunity. In fact, sometimes the rabbis "contrast the recitation of prayer with the study of the Torah to the disadvantage of the former."[24]

Early Christianity, on the other hand, adopted the policy of importunity, as illustrated in the parable of the insistent widow and the exhausted judge (Lk. 18:1–8; cf. Lk. 11:9). Paul advocates that his converts "pray without ceasing" (I Th. 5:17), and the disciples "continued steadfastly" in prayer (Lk. 24:53; Acts 1:14; 2:42; 6:4; Rom. 12:12; I Cor. 1:4). But how literally we should take all this is an open question. At any rate, the Christians seem to have observed also the more restrained Jewish tradition of regular prayers at the third, sixth, and ninth hours — at about nine in the morning, at noon, and at about three in the afternoon (Acts 2:1, 15; 3:1; 10:9) — and the Didaché states that the Lord's Prayer was said three times daily (Did. VIII, 3).

One fact is evident: that the practice of prayer became increasingly important during the intertestamental period and New Testament times. As the Jews had once counted on influencing God primarily by the temple and its sacrifices, so now, with the advancing extent of the Diaspora and finally with the destruction of the temple, they counted on influencing God by the synagogue and its prayers. Fidelity or even importunity in praying was a natural consequence. It led to a more personal relationship with a fatherly God, both in Judaism and among the Christians.[25]

---

[24] W. E. Barnes, *Early Christians at Prayer*, pp. 39, 40.

[25] As Section II, F has indicated, the inclination of many Jews and all

Finally, the spontaneous prayer is believed to be more appealing than the formula. We have already had occasion to mention the slowness with which Old Testament Judaism evolved formal prayers, and the tenacity with which it held to the spontaneous expression.[26] Sirach said: "Repeat not thy words in thy prayer" (Sir. 7:14). "In praying," said Jesus, "use not vain repetitions as the gentiles do: for they think that they shall be heard for their much speaking" (Mt. 6:7); and Rabbi Simeon advised: "When thou prayest, make not thy prayer a fixed form, but a plea for mercies, and supplications before God, for it is written, 'For he is gracious and full of compassion, slow to anger and plenteous in mercy, and repenteth him of the evil' " (Mish. Pir. Ab. 2:13, translated by Danby). As Rabbi Simeon saw quite clearly, the prayer which is spontaneous is one which will commend itself to the grace, the compassion, and the mercy of God.

Every appeal of this general category indicates a conviction that God is not merely a computer of justice: he is also a gracious Father. All who are familiar with the classic Greek religion will at once appreciate the vast difference between, on the one hand, this gentle, intimate quality of the Jewish concept of God and, on the other, the cool distance of the gods in Greek mythology. Kurt von Fritz, in his article on "Greek Prayers,"[27] accounts for the aloofness of the Hellenic gods by pointing to the devotee's fear of human arrogance; the Greek remained at a respectful distance from his gods lest he appear to consider himself their equal. Hence little mystical communion is evident in Greek prayers. The Jew, on the contrary, proceeded on the conviction that through humility and sincerity he could find God near at hand. In the spirit of a son he cried Abba and was certain that his Father heard.

Christians to resort to mediation reflects a belief in a more distant God. The two trends conflicted.

[26] See Introduction, p. 4.

[27] *Review of Religion*, X (1945), 5–39.

III. RESPONSES TO THE PRAYERS

A. A VOICE

The Old Testament describes numerous occasions on which a patriarch or a prophet conversed directly with God. When Abraham prayed, "Oh that Ishmael might live before thee!" God replied, "Behold I have blessed him, and I will make him fruitful" (Gen. 17:18, 20); Moses conversed with the voice from the burning bush (Ex. 3:4 ff.); and God and Jeremiah talked together about the drought (Jer. 14).

The documents of the intertestamental period frequently represent God as replying in an audible voice. When Ahikar prays for the birth of a son, God answers that he should rear Nadan, his sister's son (Ahik., Syr. A 1:4–6). God speaks to Moses when placing the commandments in the prophet's hand (Sir. 45:5; Jub. 1:5–18). Enoch hears the divine voice as he receives the tablets recording the history of all the generations of man (I En. 81:1); and after he has seen the awful sight of God's face, he is reassured by the words: "Have courage, Enoch; do not fear; arise and stand before my face into eternity" (II En. A 22:4, 5). God speaks audibly when he changes Jacob's name to Israel (Jub. 32:17–19). He carries on a conversation with Adam, Eve, and the serpent concerning the penalties for their respective roles in the first sin (Apoc. Mos. 23:1—29:7), and talks with the corpse of Adam about the resurrection of the flesh (Apoc. Mos. 41:1–3). Baruch often hears the voice of God explaining the mysteries of the day of judgment (II Bar. 4:1; 5:2–4; 15:1–8; 16:1—20:6; 22:1—30:5; 39:1—43:3; 49:26–41; 50:1—51:16; 76:1–4), just as Ezra hears that voice interpreting his strange visions (IV Ezra 12:10–39; 13:21–56), or speaking from a bush as to Moses (IV Ezra 14:1–26), or offering him the chalice containing the fiery water of inspiration (IV Ezra 14:38), or telling him to publish the twenty-four books of the Hebrew canon and to withhold the seventy Apocrypha for the wise (IV Ezra 14:45–47).

In the New Testament, God speaks personally in response to Jesus' prayer after baptism (Lk. 3:22) and to his prayer on the mountain of transfiguration (Lk. 9:35). Furthermore, God answers Paul's three prayers concerning "the thorn in the flesh" by saying, "My grace is sufficient for thee, for my power is made perfect in weakness" (II Cor. 12:7–9).

The audible replies to prayer are of course reminiscent of an early anthropomorphic concept of God. The Lord was once like a glorified man, so to him was attributed a human voice. The belief had its heyday in pre-exilic Judaism. In the inter-testamental writings the objective voice is often hard to distinguish from visionary experiences, and the belief is definitely on the decline in the New Testament, where none of the instances clearly involves an objective voice. Confusion on this issue of the objectivity of voices heard is especially evident in the two accounts of Saul's conversion: Acts 9:7 says specifically, "The men that journeyed with him stood speechless, hearing the voice, but beholding no man," while Acts 22:9 quotes Paul as saying, "They that were with me beheld indeed the light, but they heard not the voice of him that spake to me." In the first century A. D. this vestige of anthropomorphism is indeed faint.

B. AN ANGEL

When Hagar's child was dying of thirst in the wilderness, *God* heard the lad's cry, and an *angel* reassured Hagar so that she found the well to which *God* opened her eyes (Gen. 21:15–19). This story illustrates the vagueness of the distinction between God himself and the angels through whom he answered many a prayer. In proportion as the angel became clearly separate from God, God receded into the distance. The separation was complete and mediation well established when the angel got a name, such as Michael, Raphael, or Uriel; but even then the confusion occasionally returned, as in regard to Uriel in Fourth Ezra (IV Ezra 4:1—5:13; 7:1—9:25).

Most responses to the prayers of the Apocrypha and Pseudepigrapha came through angels. Raphael aided Tobias, Sarah, and Tobit in answer to the despairing prayers of Tobit and Sarah (Tob. 3:16, 17). In time of war, Ramiel responded by discomfiting Sennacherib's host (II Bar. 63:5–11), and celestial horsemen supported Maccabeus (II Mac. 10:25–30; 11:6–11). An angel answered Azariah's prayer by pushing back the flames of the furnace (P. Azar. 26, 27). When Abram sought guidance on his way, an angel directed him (Jub. 12:22–24). Two heavenly messengers showed mercy on the persecuted Jews and turned the frenzied elephants upon the Egyptian persecutors (III Mac. 6:17–21). In answer to the prayer against Heliodorus, a supernatural horseman and two youths struck down the blasphemer; and later they explained to him the fulfilment of the entreaty for his recovery (II Mac. 3:15–35). In the fanciful Books of Adam and Eve, prayers brought angels to aid Adam with a gift of garden land (S. L. A. E. 31:1, 2), to assist Eve in travail (L. A. E. 20:2—21:3), to explain why Adam could not have oil from the tree of life when he was in his death throes (L. A. E. 41:1—43:2), to grant Adam certain herbs from paradise (Apoc. Mos. 29:3–7), to show Adam's exalted soul to Eve (Apoc. Mos. 32:1–4), and to bury Eve beside Adam (Apoc. Mos. 43:1). But the intertestamental prayers which most frequently summoned the angels were the prayers for a revelation; thus it was that angels divulged truth to Enoch (I En. 19:1, 2; 21:1—36:4, 40:8, 9; 43:1–4; 46:1–8; 52:1—54:10; 56:2–8; 60:9, 10; 61:1–13; 71:11–17; 72:1—81:10; 108:1–15; II En. A 7:3; 8:8—22:12), to Noah (I En. 10:1, 2), to Levi (T. L. 5:5, 6), to Moses (Jub. 1:27–29), to Baruch (II Bar. 53:1—74:4; III Bar. 1:1—17:4), and to Ezra (IV Ezra 2:44–48; 4:1—5:13; 5:31—6:34; 7:1—9:25; 10:29–59).

The early Christians readily accepted the belief that God sometimes sends an angel in answer to prayer. When Zacharias prayed for a son, Gabriel came and foretold the birth (Lk. 1:13, 19, 20). On the occasion of Jesus' prayer concerning death, some of the bystanders thought they heard thunder, but others were sure that the sound was the voice of an angel replying (Jn. 12:29); and Jesus, at the time of his betrayal, trusted that, if he prayed for deliverance, God would send "more than twelve legions of angels" (Mt. 26:53). Furthermore, it was by an angel's help that Peter escaped from prison after the congregation had prayed for his safety (Acts 12:1–11; cf. Heb. 1:13, 14).

The theological implication of this belief in God's angelic agents, like the implication of the belief in man's angelic intercessors, is that God stands somewhat removed from this world, somewhat remote from man.

C. A DREAM OR VISION

When Daniel prayed for enlightenment (Dan. 10:12), God sent him a vision of a man clothed in linen, whose loins were girded with gold (Dan. 10:2–9). Probably many of the angels mentioned in the foregoing section were likewise thought of as being visions; but there is a change in the direction of sophistication when visions are clearly labeled as such. Furthermore, the concept of the vision may tend to lessen the distance between God and man, for by generating a vision in the mind of man, God is influencing man directly rather than through a mediator.

The intertestamental documents present a number of dreams and visions coming in answer to prayer. In a vision God spoke from his throne in response to Enoch's petition for the fallen angels (I En. 14:1—16:4). Levi dreamed that an angel granted his request for admittance to heaven (T. L. 2:4–6). One of Aristeas' scholars explained that God uses dreams for letting men know why their prayers are not answered (Arist. 192), and Theopompus learned through a dream the answer to his prayer asking why he had suffered madness for a time (Arist. 314, 315). Baruch's prayers brought visions for consolation and enlightenment (II Bar. 36:1; 81:2–4), and Ezra's entreaty and fasting earned the vision of weeping Zion and the dream about the man from the sea (IV Ezra 9:38—10:28; 13:1–13).

In the New Testament, Saul's prayer during his period of blindness was rewarded through a vision experienced by Ananias (Acts 9:10–16), Cornelius's prayers resulted in a vision of an angel directing him to make contact with Peter (Acts 10:1–6), and Paul's prayer in the temple brought the vision through which God bade him go out to the gentiles (Acts 22:17–21).

D. Direct Fulfilment

"Abraham prayed unto God; and God healed Abimelech and his wife and his maid-servants; and they bare children" (Gen. 20:17).

In the Apocrypha and Pseudepigrapha the direct response to prayer, while not so frequent as the response mediated by an angel, is nevertheless very much in evidence. God answers through the protection of health or through healing (Arist. 316; T. G. 5:9; IV Mac. 4:11–14); through the gift of wisdom (Wisd. 7:7); through victory in war (II Mac. 13:14–17; 15:26–34; Sir. 47:5–7), twice with the aid of a storm (Sir. 46:5; 46:16–18) and once with the aid of a bit of strategic military information whispered by human lips (I Mac. 3:44—4:4); through the miracles of the Egyptian plagues (Judith 5:12); through influencing the mind of a king (Add. Esth. 15:4–14; 15:28; Arist. 17–20; As. Mos. 4:1–6); through afflicting an enemy successively with convulsions, sleep, and forgetfulness (III Mac. 2:21, 22; 5:9–12; 5:25–28); through inspiring a young man to challenge the judges of his people (Sus. 42–46); and through the birth of a son (T. S. 2:2; T. Jud. 19:2; T. Jos. 3:7; T. B. 1:4, 5; IV Ezra 9:44, 45). The direct fulfilment of prayers in the New Testament is illustrated by the falling of the lot upon Matthias (Acts 1:24–26), by the restoration of Tabitha's life after Peter's prayer (Acts 9:40), and by the healing of Publius's father through Paul's prayer (Acts 28:8).

The direct response involves the fewest restrictions upon the concept of God. If God speaks with a voice, he is in danger of anthropomorphism. If he works through mediators or visions of mediators, men either confuse him with these mediators or think of him as holding aloof from the cosmos. But working directly, he can be universal and immanent, indwelling and transcendent.

SUMMARY

I. THE OMNIPOTENCE OF GOD

A review of the aims, inducements, and responses connected with the prayers of the intertestamental period reveals some confusion and inconsistency in Jewish thought concerning God. But there is unanimity on certain basic tenets — among them, the omnipotence of God.

In the first place, God is sovereign over the natural world. Though on occasion of dire need, as when the cisterns of beleaguered Bethulia were going dry, the devout Jew could pray for rain out of season, he seldom did so, but tacitly assumed that God would bring rain in due season as a just reward for the keeping of the Law. Prayers at mealtime acknowledged God's gracious control over all sources of food and drink.

Again, God holds sway over man's life, though he grants to man such freedom of choice as is essential to moral responsibility. Prayers for the birth of progeny reflect a conviction that God can send offspring whenever he wills to do so, even when the extreme age of the parents makes a birth possible only through a special demonstration of God's power. He can bring illness upon men and can heal. Often, though not always, sin is the provocation of physical affliction, and repentance is then the condition of release from the affliction: thus God forwards his own moral will. If he so desires, he can control even the course of a man's consciousness, inserting a dream or a vision to reveal divine intent.

From Persia came the most serious threat to the Jew's faith in God's uninterrupted sovereignty. Zoroastrianism, while asserting a conviction that the forces of light would eventually triumph over those of darkness, yielded to the arch-fiend and his hosts a temporary power over vast realms within the created world. This concession implied a clear-cut dualism running

67

through the physical world and through the moral sphere. Though many Jews of the intertestamental period accepted the widely prevalent belief in demons and in a prince of demons, all Jews stubbornly held to the prophetic conviction that God's absolute sovereignty is uninterrupted. The author of Tobit probably did not pause to weigh the theoretic question as to whether God had created the demon Asmodeus and as to whether Asmodeus was God's agent, witting or unwitting. It sufficed this writer to know that God's angel had at hand a magical practice which could vanquish the demon, and that Tobias's prayer of exorcism was effective. In evaluating the influence of Persian and Egyptian demonology upon the religion of the Jew, we must always end with a reminder that no loyal Jew could brook any real challenge to God's sovereignty. This fact is clearly attested by the very presence of prayers for exorcism.

Finally, at no point does the belief in angels become divorced from the concept of God's omnipotence. Angels serve as God's messengers, as his agents and viceroys, or as intercessors between man and God. They are subject to God's authority even if they rebel against his will. Nothing in all the religious literature of the period really compromises the dogma of omnipotence.

II. THE OMNISCIENCE OF GOD

Explicit in many of the prayers and implicit in virtually all of them is an affirmation of God's omniscience. Confident petitions for oracular responses testify to this tenet. Prayer supersedes the ancient oracular devices and strives ultimately to culminate in God's writing his wisdom, which is the Law, within the heart of man.

But certain functions assigned to God's angels might well lead a critical mind to infer that God is not thought of as being omniscient. If seven angels carry the prayers of the saints into the presence of God, and if Michael, commander of the angels, gathers up from his subordinates all the deeds of men and shows these deeds to God, God cannot be omniscient. This is not to be cited, however, as evidence of a disbelief in God's infinite wisdom; it is only an obvious instance of the theological inconsistencies of a confused era.

In fact, the Jew had never approached theology in a critical or systematic way. The genius of the Jewish faith was practical, not theoretic; and this practical character of the faith, this rooting of religion in the whole culture rather than in the subtleties of dialectic, was nowhere more evident than in the prayers of the faithful.

III. THE IMMANENCE OF GOD

Another dogma which was generally fundamental to the thought of the intertestamental period was that of the immanence of God. All the writers found God responding directly through the natural world or directly through man himself. God needed no mediator.

On the other hand, angelic agents of God's will are a commonplace throughout the period and occur in Hellenistic as well as in Palestinian sources. The belief in angels and the belief in God's immediate influence stand side by side in such documents as Second Maccabees. Furthermore, one of the latest of the Pseudepigrapha perpetuates the early Hebrew tendency to confuse an angel with God himself. Although a belief in angels should logically suggest that God is remote from our world, the Jew evidently felt no compulsion to abandon faith in God's immanence.

IV. THE OMNIPRESENCE OF GOD

Writings of this period show an underlying belief in God's omnipresence. He uses foreign nations to advance his will, and no man will escape God's final assize. Prayers for a safe journey over land or sea imply a conviction that God's presence is not limited to one small area such as the fugitive David once assigned to that presence when he said concerning his enemies, "They have driven me out this day, that I should have no share in the inheritance of Jehovah, saying, 'Go, serve other gods.' Now therefore let not my blood fall to the earth away from the presence of Jehovah" (I Sam. 26:19, 20).

However, the Jew of the Maccabean age was zealous in his assertion of God's special presence at the temple. Ancient sacred places such as Mizpah or Hebron offered man an opportunity to come closer to God than did ordinary ground; but God was nearest in the holy Zion. It is natural that this cherished belief should have been fanned to new ardor by the indignity which the Syrian oppressor Antiochus Epiphanes perpetrated by building an altar to Zeus upon the great altar in the temple. Again and again the intertestamental writers tell of urgent prayers poured out at the temple. If the petitioner could not go to that holy place, he at least faced it when he prayed, wherever he was. Such practices ran counter to the established belief in God's omnipresence; Solomon himself was reputed to have been conscious of this inconsistency at the time he dedicated the temple. But the assurance of the heart overrode the questionings of the mind. Like the idealized Solomon, the Maccabean Jew asserted God's omnipresence and yet acted as if God were present in some special way at the temple. Even Jesus, who was most insistent upon God's superiority to any limitation of place, became indignant when the temple appeared to be a "den of thieves." Since the Catholic Church finds no serious difficulty in admitting God's universal presence transcending time and place, and also his real presence in the host at the altar, we have no reason to wonder why the popular Jewish religion, which was not cautious against logical inconsistency, found no trouble at this point.

More nearly fundamental is the conflict between omnipresence and anthropomorphism. While such anthropomorphic expressions as those involving God's hand, his ear, or his eye are probably no more than literary devices,[28] one vestige of the anthropomorphic concept of God offered a more serious threat to the belief in his omnipresence: the repeated allusion to God's voice. Writers who mention his audible voice are thinking in terms of a real vestige of anthropomorphism. The voice is as prevalent

[28] For a striking exception to this statement, see Enoch's dream about God's face (II En. A 22:1–5).

in the documents of the first century A. D. as it is in the writings from the two preceding centuries and occurs not only in sources originally composed in Hebrew or Aramaic, but also in at least two which were originally Greek. Though many instances of the audible voice in apocalyptic books are part of dream experiences, the voice even then suggests a lingering influence of the anthropomorphic concept. One who consistently thinks of God as omnipresent will not assign him any of the traits of a God made in the image of man.

V. Anthropopathic Traits in the Concept of God

While the intertestamental writers generally refrained from attributing to God any physical trait of man other than an audible voice, they retained in their concept of God many of man's feelings.

God was still the warrior — often militant, sometimes manifesting hatred. The Maccabean revolt against the Seleucid tyrants inevitably intensified this human passion in the God-concept.

Secondly, on occasion God showed the spirit of the bargainer, the giver of *quid pro quo*: military victory in return for a vow of hymns, or the healing of leprosy in return for a vow to free his holy city. But many of the vows offered in this period were of a less mercenary sort, as we shall note later. The writers preferred to think of God as being superior to special inducements and as acting impartially under the terms of his fixed covenant.

In the third place, certain of the prayers imply a belief that God feels something of his own dignity, something of pride and jealousy, and a love of praise — all distinctly anthropopathic. For instance, the petitioner sometimes assigned God an attribute useful for the occasion of the prayer, then appealed to God's sense of dignity by urging him to demonstrate the attribute by answering the prayer. Others appealed to God's pride by suggesting that he let all nations know that he was God; or to his ancient jealousy by alluding to rival deities and their devotees, though monotheism was universal among the Jews. However, the most obvious appeal to God's love of praise was this suggestion: "Destroy not the mouth of them that praise thee."

A fourth example of the anthropopathic is subtler and of a higher order. To God was attributed an esthetic joy, a love of the grand pageantry of the temple ritual. Many a prayer besought him to restore or protect the temple in order that his people might utilize that ritual, and many a prayer was buttressed by the impressive pageantry and music. The Jew remembered his prophets well enough to know that the rites were futile unless joined with justice; yet God was considered esthetic as well as ethical.

VI. THE TWO FUNDAMENTAL QUALITIES OF GOD: MERCY AND JUSTICE

Despite the confusion and inconsistency that characterized the theology of the Jew in an era when he was submerged under the tidal wave generated by the grandiose Alexandrian scheme for a blend of cultures, he remained firm in his loyalty to the fundamental teaching of the great prophets concerning the nature of God: God is just and God is merciful.

These two qualities of justice and mercy are in no sense contradictory one to the other, nor are they merely complementary to each other: each is essential to the other. Without God's justice his mercy would be meaningless, for mercy is God's effort — sometimes even by chastening — to save man from the demands of justice; and without God's mercy his justice would of course degenerate into an impersonal and mechanistic order, excluding the necessity for belief in the reality of God himself. In the most turbulent of ages, Judaism remained clear on these fundamentals.

There were numerous avenues by which the petitioner approached the compassion of God. Repentance could have meant nothing to an inexorably just God; but the Jew was sure that his sackcloth and ashes, his lamentations, the beating of his breast, and the tearing of his garments, if indicative of genuine penitence, would open the door to forgiveness; and he used these same signs of mourning as an appeal to God's compassion on the occasion of urgent prayer for objectives other than pardon. Furthermore, the Jew strengthened his prayers to the merciful

God by fasting or sexual abstinence; by postures of respect, of self-abasement, or of entreaty; by the uniting of the whole congregation in the prayer or in the Amen; and by humility, earnestness, importunity, and, conversely, the avoidance of empty repetitions. While many of these practices became a means of cultivating piety in the man himself, there can be little doubt that originally they were projected toward God's mercy and that this original function remained alongside the other.

The Jewish concept of God's mercy and of the intricate involvement of that mercy in God's justice is nowhere illustrated more clearly than in the doctrine of his relationship with his chosen people. The concept of the choice arose from the doctrine of mercy, for the choice was an act of favor; but Israel's enjoyment of this favor was at once contingent upon obedience to a covenant under God's justice. Therefore, when the tyranny of Epiphanes and the revolt of Maccabeus fanned Jewish nationalism to a hot flame, and petitioners for the restoration of an independent state pled with God to remember that Israel was his chosen people, the very thought of God's ancient covenant inevitably called to the mind of the thoughtful a moral obligation on their part. The covenant was conditional. Moreover, the Jews could not forget how their prophets had warned that the foe was an instrument of God's justice toward Israel. From this realization the more idealistic Jews followed the prophets in renouncing exclusivism and in asserting that all nations would have access to the New Jerusalem, as old Tobit's prayer proclaimed. Eventually, when the Roman sword hacked down the last hope of Jewish independence, history seemed to veto Israel's nationalistic aspirations. Some of the Jews even prayed for God's protection of the world ruler, and many were sure that the justice of Israel's God and even something of God's mercy extended to every people in the circle of lands.

This justice is enduring and constant, in no way arbitrary or capricious. The Jews could be certain that, as God had wrought faithfully under his covenant in Israel's past, he would even now prove unchanging. And so in their prayers they cited great historical precedents and felt assured that God would not alter his ways.

The implication of prayers of confession is that man's sin constitutes an offense against God, who is devoted to righteousness. In the character of God this devotion to righteousness is so basic that God's wisdom is identified with the Law. Some of the most elevated prayers have as their object the worshiper's progressive acquisition of this wisdom, that God's Law may be written in the worshiper's heart. In one of the latest of the Pseudepigrapha, as in Paul's letters, this inward Law is known as God's Holy Spirit, which makes for righteousness.

Because of this conviction that God is the well-spring of righteousness, numerous petitioners turned to him for the gift of specific virtues or for protection from future sin. When they prayed God to deliver them from temptation by evil spirits or by the evil one, they evidenced a feeling that God in his righteousness could not tempt man. Such prayers seem to lose sight of God's sovereignty while defending his righteousness.

Intertestamental prayers reveal a clash of ideas as to when and how God will fulfil the demands of his justice, but the very existence of this clash underlines the conviction that God's justice will be satisfied. Some Jews, even to the end of the period, held to the conventional belief that God enforces justice here and now, delivering or mercifully chastening the righteous man and scourging the unrighteous. However, since the reward of the righteous under this point of view included material prosperity, the hope seemed vain to those who, like Job, had experienced unmerited misfortune.

This disillusionment led increasing numbers of Jews to incline toward the more distant hope foreshadowed in the closing chapters of Daniel, probably the latest book destined to be included in the Hebrew canon. In his own good time God would intervene mightily to establish a kingdom of justice. Men who died before the coming of this cataclysm would rise from their graves to be judged, and only the righteous would share in the new world. But Jews who had accepted the foreign concept of a soul that survives the death of the body were convinced that God's justice would assert itself immediately after the death of the individual. Souls of the good entered at once into a blissful state, and those of the wicked experienced torment. This belief did not make its way into the religious literature until late in the period and was therefore likely to combine itself with the earlier belief concerning an ultimate resurrection of the body.

Thus far we have considered prayers aimed at the establishing of justice; it remains to summarize inferences drawn from prayers the aim of which is something other than the establishing of justice, but which employ as their inducement an appeal to God's justice. An obvious example is the vow of some righteous act in return for an answer to the prayer, the implication being that God values righteousness. Similar is the implication of the belief that God answers the prayers of men whose lives on the whole are upright. The man who gives with generosity will receive freely from God; the man who forgives will be fogiven; the man who labors to bring his own prayer to pass is assured of God's aid. For God is just.

But is God's judgment influenced by factors other than the deeds of the individual man? Prayers of the period reveal a sharp division of opinion among the Jews concerning the old question as to whether the sins and merits of the fathers have a bearing upon God's dealings with subsequent generations. If the fathers have eaten sour grapes, are the children's teeth set on edge? To change the figure and also suggest the converse, can men draw from a reservoir of merit stored up by others? Despite the protests recorded in the prophecies of Ezekiel and Jeremiah and echoed by more than one of the intertestamental writers, petitioners continued to ask God for favor in the light of their forefathers' merit.

Closely related is the belief that God heeds the prayers of martyrs who ask him to accept their virtuous suffering as an atonement for the shortcomings of others. Moreover, innumerable prayers from the period rely upon the influence of a meritorious intercessor. As in the Old Testament, this intercessor may be a prophet, a priest, a scribe, or any other upright man whose superior goodness might move God to grant the request; but in the Apocrypha and Pseudepigrapha the intercessor is more likely to be an angel. The effectiveness of intercession, like that of an appeal to the fathers' merit, was evidently a controversial issue. Two of the later writers of the period warn

sternly that no intercessor, however meritorious, will be able
to stand forward for a man at the final judgment; everyone will
have to face the consequences of his own deeds.

Thus, while the Apocrypha and Pseudepigrapha are unan-
imous in ascribing to God perfect justice, they disagree as to
how God's justice proceeds. Does God judge each man on his
own merit, or does God's mercy permit a sharing of superfluous
merit? Does God balance the books here and now, or will his
justice complete its demands later? If later, will the rewards
and punishments await a grand assize when the very bodies of
all the dead will rise from their graves, or will a just compensation
overtake each individual immediately after death, when a soul
surviving the body enters into rest or torment? Possibly both
alternatives would prove true, and the risen bodies would meet
the surviving souls on the last day. But the most crucial issue
was the clash between nationalism and universalism. Does God's
mercy extend beyond his own people, or do the gentiles face
only a relentless justice? These were the questions with which
the Jew was struggling as he pondered the justice and compassion
of God.

VII. CONCLUSION

An analytic study of the Jewish concept of God is liable to
do injustice to the religion of the Jew unless we constantly remind
ourselves that these dry bones live. Our discussion of the Jew's
implied attitude toward God's omniscience, immanence, and
omnipresence; our detection of certain anthropomorphic or
anthropopathic traits in the Jew's delineation of Jehovah; our
analysis of just how the Jew thought God's justice and mercy
dealt with the chosen people and with the gentile world — all
these technical considerations bear somewhat the same relation
to historical Judaism as an anatomist's sketches bear to a living
body. The Jew was not a theologian. His was a practical
religion which had grown out of a struggle extending through two
thousand years, and out of an undying conviction that God had
alloted Israel a great function to fulfil. Through famine and
enslavement, defeat and deportation, in the face of the desecra-

tion of what he revered and the collapse of the national hope
he cherished, the Jew persistently revised his thinking, sometimes with inconsistency, but always so as to retain the covenant
binding Israel to God and shaping the daily life of the Jew.
Through an increasing practice of prayer this relationship between God and the man who kept God's Law, deepened into a
rich mysticism. Without an appreciation of this inward vitality
of a moral faith, our critical studies misrepresent the religion
of the Jew in the years between the Testaments.

www.ingramcontent.com/pod-product-compliance
Lightning Source LLC
LaVergne TN
LVHW041206080426
835508LV00008B/819